A Letter from Ireland: Volume 2

Mike Collins lives in County Cork, Ireland. He travels around the island of Ireland with his wife, Carina, taking pictures and listening to stories about families, names and places. He and Carina share these pictures and stories at:

www.YourIrishHeritage.com

He also writes a weekly Letter from Ireland, which is sent out to people of Irish ancestry all over the world. This volume is the second collection of those letters.

A Letter from Ireland: Volume 2

Irish Surnames, Counties, Culture and Travel

Mike Collins

Your Irish Heritage.

First published 2014 by

Your Irish Heritage

Email: mike@youririshheritage.com

Website: www.youririshheritage.com

CREDITS

All photographs and illustrative materials are the author's own.

The publisher gratefully acknowledges the many individuals who granted A Letter from Ireland permission to reprint the cited material.

ISBN:9781505438628

DESIGN

Cover design by Ian Armstrong, Onevision Media

Your Irish Heritage,

Old Abbey, Cork, Ireland

PRAISE FOR 'A LETTER FROM IRELAND'

It's a great book for those, like myself, who have read a great deal about the history in which my ancestors live but still scratch their heads feeling like there's something missing. Mike fills in many of those gaps in interesting and thought provoking ways, making you crave more.

Edward Reidy

If you have Irish blood running through your veins, or even if you're just interested in Ireland, this book is essential.

Patty McCoy

This book is a gem (or should I say an emerald)........scholarship wrapped in plain English. The book is essential reading for anyone with Irish blood in their veins.

Simon O'Flynn

Mike writes in a wonderfully conversational way that is easy to digest, regardless of the subject matter. If you're looking for an easily digestible overview of Irish history and the evolution of Irish surnames, this is a great place to start.

Joe Estadt

I found it to be extremely well researched and presented. The explanations of names and places are outstanding. This is not a difficult read, but it is worth any effort just to get the sense of Ireland. I learned a great deal, not only about the origins of my family's name but of the geography from which they came. The local colour is outstanding. If you have a drop of Irish in you, you will benefit from reading this book.

Patricia Burgess

This book gives you an idea of how things came to be in bygone eras of Ireland. Infused with a bit of humour to keep you smiling along the way, the past is explained and surnames broken down to help answer questions in a search for a family's past. It's delightful, informative and a great read, so kick back with your cup of coffee or tea, and let Mike take you into your past.

Nancy Webster

A wonderful read! A must for anyone interested in Irish ancestry! Family names and places offer so much information and insight!

Kathy Mandato

If you are a student of Irish history, genealogy, surname studies and things of this nature, this book is sure to hit your interests. It examines surnames in their proper linguistic and historical context, and helps point the reader in the right direction for further study, making it a valuable resource in its own right. I highly recommend it.

Tracy Tucker

This book is a Treasure. I have read, or I should say, I have started to read several books on Irish history. Never finished any of them. This book is a pleasure to read and a wealth of great information. My ancestors have come to life. Mike writes in a way that is humorous, insightful, and extremely *interesting. I highly recommend 'A Letter from Ireland'.*

Sandra Laferriere

I very much enjoyed reading this book and found it very touching how it inspired a heartfelt sense of kinship with people of Irish connection both in Ireland and all over the world. It is short, but sweet! I highly recommend it.

Reginald Murphy

This is an easy to read history of the clans, tribes and kings of Ireland. A must for amateur genealogists. Rekindled my desire to connect with my ancestors.

Mary Leidner

Great book; it felt like I was traveling through Ireland with the author. Can't wait for the next book!

Judy Simmons

DEDICATION

This book is dedicated to the forty million plus people of Irish descent around the world—and the tens of thousands of these who read 'A Letter from Ireland' and make the journey so wonderfully worthwhile.

Contents

Preface

Why write a second volume of 'A Letter from Ireland'? Maybe it's best to answer that question with a letter or two! Here is a letter I received only last month from one Mary Walsh—but it is so representative of many of the letters that I receive each week.

'Dear Mike,

Maybe you can help me. I have reached a brick wall with research on my Great Great Grandfather—Patrick Dempsey. He was born in Ireland about 1820, but I can find no records of his location, birth or any other facts about his life before arrival in the U.S. I have spoken with all my living relatives (the ones that I know of) and have already employed two Genealogists, but they were unable to uncover any new information. Can you help?'

Mary Walsh.

Maybe you know Mary's frustration yourself? You know, you may trace your Irish family tree in many directions, but no matter how much time, effort (and money) you put into it—you just can't get beyond a certain point.

Here is my reply back to Mary:

'Dear Mary,

That must be so frustrating to actually have a name and a connection—but to feel that Patrick's past is lost in a haze somewhere back in Ireland of the early 1800s. However, many people of Irish descent hit a 'brick wall' such as yours, sooner or later. Maybe you'll get around this obstacle with hard work

1

and some luck, but most likely you'll eventually hit a final wall. You reach the end of the available record trail. Then what?

I started to write the 'Letter from Ireland' shortly after I noticed people asking questions about their Irish surnames, and trying to interpret Irish records, on some internet forums. I was surprised to realise just how many answers I could supply—a lot of which come from a familiarity and passion for Irish history, the Irish language, customs and traditions. Those of us brought up in Ireland often know more about these things than we realise.

The 'Letter from Ireland' is sent out each week and covers a different aspect of Irish culture, tradition, family surnames and the odd bit of craic! Shortly after we began, people started to write back. Some asked short questions—and some people supplied long and fantastic family stories that you would have trouble believing in a book of fairy tales. But they were real.

I noticed that once a person 'relaxed' a little about getting the full measure of their ancestors—the dates of birth (many alternatives!), marriages, number of children and eventual place of burial—they then started to become more interested in discovering the actual Irish life of their ancestors. They wanted to know about the music, traditions, words and celebrations that grounded their ancestors in the country around them.

This is what we cover each week on a Letter from Ireland. We focus on that rich world of living Irish culture and tradition that produced your ancestors— and many of the resulting attitudes and beliefs that probably guide you through each day. We aim to go beyond genealogy. And when we go there, I ask that you please do hold on to your precious ancestry records—but let's make them dance into your life in a way that makes you smile each day at the treasure you have inherited to share with those all around you.

Yours for now—and I look forward to chatting soon,

A Chara, Mike.'

So, now we have arrived at the second volume of 'A Letter from Ireland'—which is a collection of the letters from Ireland written each Sunday morning over the last year. You will notice the writing follows an informal and chatty style—I decided to keep this style throughout the book as it seems to work best for all our readers— and I do hope that works for you too.

The letters in this book will give you a better sense of what Mary Walsh and I talked about in the exchange above. We aim to go beyond genealogy and to develop a better sense of the lives, times and challenges of your Irish ancestors.

Finally, you might know my fondness for the oral Irish tradition of the 'seanfhocal', or wise saying. Here is one that captures the sentiment of all the words I have used so far in a much lighter fashion:

'Is buaine port ná glór na n-éan,

Is buaine focal ná toice an tsaoil.'

'A tune outlasts the song of the birds,

A word outlasts the wealth of the world.'

What a very Irish sentiment! The values and priorities of an Irish Heritage wrapped up in two lines!

As you read through the Letters in this book, I look forward to hearing back from you—and sharing the surnames, stories and traditions in your Irish family tree.

Mike Collins,
Cork, Ireland,
November 2014.

This book was shaped by the many comments and questions from our wonderful readers—and I do hope you enjoy it. If you would like to connect with us even further, feel free to sign up for our 'Letter from Ireland' at:

www.youririshheritage.com/letterfromireland

Introduction

I never realised that I would be writing the introduction to this book, 'A Letter from Ireland: Volume 2' so soon after the release of Volume 1. Each Sunday morning I send out the 'Letter'—and hour later I receive the first of many replies. The family stories, yarns and myths contained in these replies inspire future issues of a Letter from Ireland, and so a wondrous positive loop of communication is sustained between all us correspondents.

In this volume, I am delighted to include just some of those wonderful stories submitted by our readers. I think you will agree that this is a trend we should continue, and increase, for the future.

We are now almost into two years of the Letter—and it is becoming plain the sorts of themes that appear on a regular basis. So, as in Volume One, I have created a number of categories and placed each letter in the appropriate one. The sections are as follows:

Section 1. Your Irish Surname

Each time we get a new reader on the 'Letter from Ireland', I ask for the Irish surnames in their family tree. This is the 'token' that we use to track much of an individual's Irish ancestry. It gives the best clues as to which county your family came from in Ireland, their likely ancient origins as well as how that name ties in with other Irish surnames in the locality.

In this section we look at the wider stories of your Irish surname and the places and family groups associated with that name.

Section 2: A Trip to Ireland

Carina and I spend a lot of our year travelling around Ireland—taking pictures and gathering stories to share. Since we started the letter, we realised just how many of our readers travel to Ireland on a regular basis as well as just how many armchair travellers we have in the group! In this section we explore places, counties and itineraries. We suggest the best places to tour when you want to take in the culture and heritage of Ireland as well as exploring the Ireland of your ancestry.

Section 3: The Irish Diaspora

The word 'Diaspora' has come into common use over the past number of decades. In the case of Ireland, it refers to the many people of Irish ancestry who now reside across the globe. It is estimated that there are about eighty million such people—many with a significant affiliation to the Irish culture and attitudes that spread from our small island over many hundreds of years. Here we look at just some of those 'places of the Diaspora' and a number of unique family stories.

Section 4: Culture, Customs, Music and Craic

I think most people will agree that 'Irishness' comes down to a mix of these four words (with some red hair thrown in for good measure!). We are fortunate as a race that so many aspects of our custom and culture travelled so far and lasted for so long. Some people talk about 'genetic memory'—a sense of Irishness that just seems to live within them, but many of our traditions had already lasted for hundreds of years before the first large emigrations.

Section 5: Our Reader's Letters from Ireland

It is such a privilege to include these Letters! So many talented individuals put pen to paper and either remembered or imagined a trip to Ireland. Here we see just a few examples of the wonderful results.

Appendix: The Surnames of Your Irish Heritage.

Finally, when our readers sign up for the 'Letter from Ireland', we ask you to share the Irish surnames in their family tree and the counties these names came from originally. This allows us to put together a large database of Irish surnames and their counties of origin. We use this information to put together many of the facts and observations mentioned in the 'Letter from Ireland'.

In this section, I have reproduced all of the names currently on our list (maybe it includes yours?)—including their last known Irish county of residence.

I do hope you enjoy this collection of Letters from Ireland.

Slán for now, Mike.

Section 1: Your Irish Surname

The Healys and Finding Your Ancestral Home

May 18, 2014

Céad Míle Fáilte from County Cork—and I hope you are keeping well wherever you are. It's a bit drizzly looking out the window this morning, but I can't complain as we've had a great spell of dry weather over the last few weeks.

I'm having a nice cup of pure Cork tea (it does exist!) to warm up the insides—so why don't you have a cup of whatever you fancy and join me for today's letter.

Finding Your Ancestral Home.

I often get mails from people wondering about their ancestral Irish homelands (and homestead if possible, please!). Sometimes my answer points them in a specific direction and sometimes my answer is a little more vague.

This week I want to share Jack Healey's story with you. He contacted me last week to share the following:

'My wife and I visited Ireland in 2012 for the first time for a 25th wedding anniversary tour with Wild West Irish Tours (Mike says: I have heard good things about this group so I am happy to share the name). The tour focused on County Sligo and it's so beautiful! We hope to return someday soon for a much longer stay and more extensive immersion in the history and culture of Ireland.

My great-great grandfather, Michael Healy, immigrated to the US in the mid-1800s, but I know very little except for the scant footprint he left. But I do at least have the census record of his national origin to work from. Maybe someday we'll learn more of his roots in Ireland.'

First, Jack, I'm delighted that you and your wife had such a memorable anniversary and second—thanks for agreeing to let me publish your letter here. You see, Jack's story reminded me of the complications around Irish ancestry research—so I wanted to share a few perspectives with him—and everyone else who reads this letter.

You see, Jack and his wife may have unknowingly toured only a few miles from his ancestral home.

The Problem with Irish Names.

Tracing your Irish Ancestry can be really complicated! I have written quite a lot on the origins of your Irish surname—let's take the example of Jack and his story.

If you look up the name Healey/Healy you will probably find that it is an Anglo-Saxon surname from Lancashire in England. But that sort of information is usually misleading when your ancestor comes from Ireland. That's the problem with sites like Ancestry.com—they are great for records but often misleading when it comes to Irish ancestry information.

In Ireland, the surname Healy (or Hely or Healihy) is normally a phonetic translation of a couple of Irish language surnames:

- Ó hÉalaighthe from County Cork
- Ó hÉilidhe from County Sligo

When I say 'phonetic' translation I mean that if I said these names to you in Irish—you would hear 'Oh Heela' and you may then 'peg' this sound to a name with which you are already familiar (e.g. Healy) or simply spell the name the way you hear it in English.

These were two distinct families of Healys descended from two different ancestors. In Cork they came from the Donoghmore area in the north of the county—and in Sligo they came from Ballyhealy (imagine that!) near the Curlew mountains on the shores of Lough Arrow.

I do like to think that he was only a few miles from his ancestral Healy homeland as he celebrated his 25th wedding anniversary on his first visit to Ireland. What do you think?

Maybe he'll head back there over the next few years to soak up the sights and sounds of the Healy clan—a leading family of County Sligo up to the time of Cromwell in the mid-1600s.

That's it for now!

Slán, Mike... talk next week! :)

The Most Numerous Irish Surname

May 25, 2014

Céad Míle Fáilte from County Cork—and I do hope you are doing well wherever you are. It's a long weekend for our readers in both the US and the UK, but I'm not that jealous as we had our own holiday a couple of weeks back.

We were up early dropping our daughter off to the plane for a summer of working in San Diego. The house is quiet at the moment with all of our children now away outside Ireland. I'm back on the Barry's tea this morning, so why don't you have a cup of whatever you fancy and join me for today's letter?

The response to last week's letter was truly amazing with so many people sharing stories of their visits to Ireland and finding the places that link to their ancestors. In fact, over the last month we have had quite a few success stories come through both from this Letter and the Green Room (our members area)—stories that tell of finding a house or a photograph or a headstone or a relative at the end of a family search. We really must share some more of these stories in the near future.

One Tribe of Ireland.

Last week a man named David Fallon did me a good deed—and of course, no good deed goes unpunished! David did not realise that I am in the habit of looking at a surname, uncovering the story behind it, and sharing it on this letter!

The surname Fallon comes from the Irish 'Ó Fallamhain'—which pretty much sounds like the English version when you say it in Irish. It came from County Roscommon, just west of the town of Athlone (although a smaller group came from Offaly also). They were one of the main clans of the larger tribe of the Uí Maine. The Uí Maine were a people who descended from a common ancestor—Maine Mór in the 5th century—and lived in an area covering modern east County Galway and a large part of County Roscommon.

A small point—when you see Uí—that is the plural of 'of', so 'Uí' means 'descendants of'. The singular—'Ua'—means 'descendant of'. Over the years this has been replaced by 'Ó' or just 'O'—and so we have all those modern Irish surnames like O'Connor and so on.

End of lesson!

The Most Numerous Irish Surname in the World.

As I mentioned, the Fallons were one of the surnames that came out of the Uí Maine over the centuries. Other families include:

O'Donnellan, O'Madden, O'Concannon, O'Coffey, O'Naughten, O'Mulally, MacKeogh, MacGeraghty, O'Fahy, O'Downey, O'Dugan, O'Kenny, O'Murray, O'Tracy, O'Connolly, O'Conry, O'Drennan, O'Dolan, O'Mannion, MacWard, O'Lennon, Cashin and MacGing/MacGinn.

Are any of your Irish names here? However, there is one other surname—and it is often cited as the most numerous Irish surname in the world today—Kelly.

The O'Kellys of the Uí Maine.

While Kelly can also have a source in other parts of Ireland, Scotland and England—I think it's safe to say that the majority of the 500,000 or so Kellys around the world today have a link to the homelands of the Uí Maine. If you travel to the village of Knockcroghery in County Roscommon—and venture to the ruins of Gailey Castle on the shores of Lough Ree—you will look at what was the seat of the Kelly lords for many centuries.

The Kellys took their name from one illustrious ancestor called 'Ceallach', who was King of Uí Maine in 874 AD. The name in Irish is 'Ó Ceallaigh'—meaning 'descendant of Ceallach'. Since the 1600s, with the ascendency of the English in Ireland, the Kellys have been scattered all over Ireland—many to the other counties of Connaught such as Mayo.

Maybe you have a Kelly or two in your family tree? Maybe you have a relative with the first name of Kelly? I'm sure you know of many cultural icons with a surname of Kelly—such as Grace and Gene?

That's it for now!

Slán, Mike... talk next week! :)

The Warrior Surnames of Ireland

October 5, 2014

Céad Míle Fáilte—and welcome to your Letter from Ireland. Well now, the weather has really changed over the week here in County Cork. We have high winds, sharp air and a threat of local flooding. And just last Sunday we were swimming in the sea!

I do hope you are keeping well wherever you are today. I'm having a nice cup of Lyon's tea this morning—the tea my mother weaned us onto when we were toddlers! So, I hope you'll have a cup of whatever you fancy yourself and join me for today's letter.

The Warrior Surnames of Ireland.

A few weeks back, I received the following mail from Brenda Mills—one of our regular readers:

'I would love to know more about the McCoys and where they came from. My grandmother would only say the McCoys were from Ireland. When I was in Ireland, I was in Blarney Woollen Mills and there was an author selling his book. He told me that the McCoys were from Ulster. I have not been able to prove that one way or the other. Any info would help.'

Well, Brenda, I could tell you that the surname McCoy comes from the Irish 'Mac Aodha' and leave it at that. However, there is a much bigger story behind the McCoys in Ulster—and a number of similar distinct surnames found around Ireland. You see, the McCoys of Ulster were a 'Galloglass' family.

If you enjoy a little Shakespeare from time to time, you may have come across the following words in his play 'Macbeth':

'The merciless Macdonald,
Worthy to be a rebel, for to that
The multiplying villainies of nature
Do swarm upon him, from the Western isles
Of kerns and gallowglasses is supplied'

The term 'Gallowglass' mentioned comes from the Irish 'Gallóglaigh' which literally translates as 'young foreign warrior'. This is a name that the Irish gave to those Norse-Scottish mercenaries who appeared on Irish shores for the first time in the 1200s. They came from the part of Scotland that was once the Kingdom of the Dal Riada—a kingdom that spread between the north of Ireland and the west of Scotland.

As Scots, they were Gaelic and shared a common culture and language with the Irish. But since they had intermarried with the Norse settlers in Scotland, the Irish called them 'Gall Gaeil' ('foreign Gaels'). Many of the families in this area had become effective warriors, developing superior fighting methods and technology to that of the Irish.

The Arrival of the Norse-Gaels in Ireland.

Over in Ireland the Irish chieftains were facing a new and deadly threat. The Normans arrived in Ireland in the late 1100s, and after a difficult start, established a series of strongholds across the country into the 1200s.

The Irish chieftains faced a number of problems in fighting off this Norman threat to their Irish lands: First, the Normans easily beat the Irish forces in direct and open combat with their superior fighting methods and technology. Second, Irish society was made up of a series of alliances that could unravel at any time. An ally could suddenly join the Normans for a particular fight to gain the upper hand over a neighbour. The Gallowglass warriors of the western isles of Scotland provided a solution to both of these problems.

The first recorded Gallowglass arrival in Ireland was in 1259 AD, when the King of Connacht was provided with one hundred and sixty of these soldiers. They were provided with land and received supplies from the local lordships.

They carried a two-handed axe and a broadsword—and wore chainmail with an iron helmet—all of which were new to the native Irish. This equipment, as well as their fighting approach, made them more suitable for direct battle with the Normans (the native Irish typically made more use of their knowledge of local woods and bogs to ambush and skirmish). The local chiefs also felt comfortable with the loyalty of the Gallowglass as they were less affected by local feuds and promises.

So, how did some of the Gallowglass surnames become so prominent in Ireland?

Well, some of these Gallowglass families were on the losing side of the Scottish wars of independence and this meant the complete loss of their lands. When they were offered alternative lands in Ireland in return for service, many decided to migrate as a full family group. The first of these clans were the MacSweeneys, who settled in Donegal. These were followed by MacDonnells/ McDonalds in Antrim and the MacCabes in Cavan.

By 1512AD, there were about 60 Galloglass groups around the country under the Irish lords. They may have started out as Norse-Scots mercenary groups—but settled over time and intermarried with the native Irish. The term Gallowglass came to mean more a 'fighting unit' that consisted of men of many different backgrounds. These Gallowglasses were an important part of the Irish fighting force right up to the Battle of Kinsale in 1601AD.

The Fighting Norse-Scots-Irish Surnames.

As I mentioned previously, whole Galloglass families left Scotland to settle in Ireland. So, although some of these surnames originated in Scotland, they are now considered Irish and include the following surnames:

McCabe, McCallion/McCallan, McColl/McColley, McCrory/ McRory/Rogers, Gallogly/English, McGirr/Short, McGreal, Sheehy, McSorley and McSweeney/McSwiney.

When these surnames are found in Scotland today, it's often due to later Irish catholic emigration from Ireland to Scotland after the Irish famine.

However, a larger number of Galloglass families came to Ireland only on a seasonal basis—or only parts of their clan moved fully to Ireland. As a result, there are a number of Gallowglass surnames that could be considered both Irish and Scottish—and are still found in both Ireland and Scotland today. These include:

McAllister/McAlister, McAteer/McIntyre, McAuley/ McAulay/ McCauley, Campbell, McClean/McLean, McCoy/McKay, McCollum/McCallum, McDowell/McDougall (some became Doyle), McDonnell/McDonald, McFadden/McFayden and McNeill.

Remember that these Gallowglass surnames arrived in Ireland from Scotland before the reformation. However, from the 17th century on—some of these surnames also arrived in Ulster as planted settlers—now typically Presbyterian.

So, Brenda—it seems like your friend in Blarney Woolen Mills was right—the McCoys in Ireland are typically from Ulster and most arrived in Ireland as warriors with fighting on their mind!

That's it for this week.

Slán for now, Mike :)

The Tribes of Galway

October 19, 2014

Céad Míle Fáilte—and welcome to your Letter from Ireland. We're 'playing a blinder' given the time of year here in Ireland—the weather is staying mild (just very windy as the leaves come floating down). The warmer temperatures should shorten the winter very nicely. I do hope the weather is treating you well wherever you are today!

I'm having a nice cup of peppermint tea this morning, and I do hope you'll have a cup of whatever you fancy and join me for today's letter.

Have you ever noticed that when people talk about Irish names, they often use words like 'clan' or 'sept' or sometimes even 'tribe' (one of my favourites) to describe particular groups of families? Well, this morning we are going to have a look at one particular group of 'Tribes' in Ireland.

Swings, Roundabouts and Tribal Names.

A few weeks back, we headed north from Cork to the city of Galway and nearby Connemara. What a beautiful part of the world—maybe you have been there?

One of the first things you notice on approaching Galway city is the series of traffic roundabouts that dot its' periphery. These fourteen roundabouts have a family name planted in the middle of each—names such as Kirwan, Blake, D'Arcy and so on. These are the surnames that belong to the 'Tribes of Galway'.

Helen Blake from Australia was on to me recently with the following introduction:

'Hi Mike, thank you for the newsletter. I am a descendant of the Blake family of Menlo in Galway and Towerhill, Co. Mayo. My Menlo connection goes back to the 3rd Baronet. Then the family branched off to Towerhill, my GGGG Grandfather being Isidore Maurice Blake of Towerhill and Oldhead. The Blakes of Menlo Castle, Co. Galway, held the lands of Clonyne and Clooneen or Towerhill, parish of Touaghty, barony of Carra, Co. Mayo. My GG Grandfather Dr Isidore Maurice Blake came to Australia in 1842.'

Isn't it a privilege (and so rare)—as I remarked to Helen—to have so much Irish lineage recorded for future generations? Now, while Helen mentions Menlo Castle above, if you head into the centre of Galway city, you will also find a medieval townhouse known as 'Blake's Castle'. You see, the Blake family were one of the fourteen 'Tribes of Galway'.

The Tribes of Galway.

A fort was built where Galway city now stands in 1124 AD. It was erected by Turlough O'Connor—King of Connaught at the time—on land controlled by the local O'Halloran family. However, it soon came under successful attack by the local (and fierce) O'Flahertys who assumed control of the area.

About one hundred years after the building of this fort, the Normans arrived in Connaught in the shape of the de Burgo family (the modern surname Burke). Richard Mór de Burgh captured Galway fort in 1232 and established a small walled town which he proceeded to 'plant' with merchant and craft families. Over the next hundred years, Galway grew and thrived under the Burkes, establishing a reputation as an important trading port. However, in 1333, the town of Galway broke away from the in-fighting Burkes, and received the first stage of a royal charter in 1396.

The town eventually became ruled by a group of fourteen merchant families—each taking it in turn to assume Mayoral duties. One of Helen's ancestors—John Blake fitz William became the third mayor of Galway in 1487.

The merchant family names were: Athy, Blake, Bodkin, Browne, D'Arcy, Deane, Font, French, Joyce, Kirwan, Lynch, Martin, Morris and Skerrett. Twelve of these families were of Anglo-Norman origin while two were Irish Gaelic in origin (D'Arcy and Kirwan).

Galway became a prosperous and strategically important town—at one time it was the main port for trade with France and Spain on the Island. Relationships between the residents of Galway and their Gaelic and Norman (but Gaelicised) neighbours were rarely 'quiet'. Indeed, the following prayer was hung over the west gate of the city—facing the territory of that same clan:

From the Ferocious O'Flahertys may God protect us

Galway took the side of royalist Catholic forces in the Confederate wars from 1641—and when Cromwell arrived in Ireland to punish the losing Catholic side, he granted the merchant families in Galway the derogatory nickname of the 'Tribes of

Galway'. The families decided to hang onto this nickname in that typical Irish mixture of defiance and contradictory respect.

The town of Galway was besieged by Cromwell's forces and the residents surrendered in April of 1652. Following this, the ruling 'Tribes' lost much of their power and were replaced by local protestant families.

However, some of the families held onto land across the Counties of Galway and Mayo, and by the time the monarchy was restored in the 1690s they were rewarded for their loyalty with a partial restoration of their power, titles and lands. It is these families, like the Blakes, that have maintained lineages and genealogies to the present day.

These family names—Martin, Lynch, Blake, French and Joyce— are found in quantity across the counties of Galway and Mayo today, mixed in with the O'Flaherty, O'Halloran and Burke surnames. You will also find many descendants of these families living in Australia as we write—neighbours of Helen Blake and her own 'Tribe of Galway'.

Do any of your Irish family names descend from the Tribes of Galway?

That's it for this week.

Slán for now, Mike :)

Section 2: A Trip to Ireland

The Wild Ancestry Way

August 24, 2014

Céad Míle Fáilte—and welcome to your Letter from Ireland on a rainy Sunday morning here in County Cork. The weather has changed in these parts—and the mornings and evenings have definitely become chillier. On the other hand, we're enjoying the blackberries and apples that show up this month—definitely a star crop this year! I hope the weather is treating you well wherever you are.

I'm having a nice cup of Badger and Dodo coffee this morning for a kick-start—don't you just love the name—and I do hope you'll have a cup of whatever you fancy as you join me for today's Letter.

After last week's letter on 'McCarthy's Bar' and planning a trip around Ireland, I received SO MANY responses, stories and suggestions. It became clear just how many of us are dreaming of, planning or even in the middle of a trip around this island as we speak.

So, this week we will stay on the theme of travelling around Ireland—but with an ancestry focus.

The Wild Atlantic Ancestry Way.

Have you heard of the 'Wild Atlantic Way'? This is the name given to a new drive all along the west coast of Ireland. It was launched earlier this year and ties together some of the most beautiful scenery in the world into one of Europe's longest scenic drives.

This year, Carina and I decided to undertake the drive for ourselves. Maybe you have been following our progress on our Facebook page? If you head over to the Wild Atlantic Way page on our blog, you can see the sections we have already travelled—and what has yet to come. Maybe you have travelled some of these sections yourself?

Now, while the drive is being promoted for the wonderful scenery along the way, as well as lots of healthy outdoor pursuits— we undertook the journey for a slightly different reason. Let me explain.

A Journey into the Ireland of Your Ancestors.

One of the things we do when you sign up for the 'Letter from Ireland' is ask about the Irish surnames in your family and the counties you think they came from. Over the last 18 months, we have gathered about 10,000 names into our database.

The Wild Atlantic Way travels along 8 of Ireland's 32 counties— it includes Counties Cork, Kerry, Clare, Galway, Mayo, Sligo, Leitrim and Donegal. If we look at our list of your Irish surnames, the following is a breakdown of where they came from:

- 15.6% of our reader ancestors came from County Cork

- 5.5% of our reader ancestors came from County Kerry

- 5.7% of our reader ancestors came from County Clare

- 5.3% of our reader ancestors came from County Galway

- 9.1% of our reader ancestors came from County Mayo

- 2.6% of our reader ancestors came from County Sligo

- 1.7% of our reader ancestors came from County Leitrim

- 5.6% of our reader ancestors came from County Donegal

In total, 51.1% of our reader's Irish ancestors came from the counties along the Wild Atlantic Way. Why is this?

OK, it is true that the Way contains some of the largest counties in Ireland. However, along with providing some of the most beautiful rugged scenery in the world, this whole area was hugely over-populated by the 1840s. There was one food source that thrived on the poor land to the west of these counties and that enabled the relocated Gaelic Irish to thrive and multiply. This food source was the potato.

Of course, many of us know what happened next. Successive potato crop failures brought about the great famine in the 1840s over much of Ireland (known in Irish as 'an Gorta Mór' or the 'Great Hunger'). This triggered over a million deaths and the emigration of a million others. The counties of the west of Ireland made up a significant majority of these Irish Gaelic emigrants. Maybe your ancestors were among them?

I strongly recommend you try and view the book: *'Atlas of the Great Irish Famine'* in a library, or buy it as a treat for yourself. It is expensive—but incredible value as it offers an amazing insight into what life was like for your ancestors at the time of An Gorta Mór, along with so many of the local county histories.

So, Carina and I decided to travel the Wild Atlantic Way with this history in mind. As we travel along, we talk about the folk history of the area, the music and traditions, the towns and family surnames associated with each—as well as showing pictures of an incredibly beautiful landscape—a landscape that must have been so hard to work and live off for many of our Irish ancestors. This is a landscape that has suffered from emigration from the 1840s all the way to the 1950s and beyond.

Take the example of just one of the smaller counties, County Leitrim. Today, Leitrim has a population of 33,470. In the 1841 census, the population was about 105,000. A drop in population of almost 70%.

On the Wild Atlantic Way, you will often travel through very isolated areas—and notice the abandoned cottages and whole abandoned villages around you. This landscape tells the story of our Irish ancestors. A story that is hard to ignore.

So, that's the story that we are exploring on our journey along Ireland's Wild Atlantic Way.

Do head over to www.youririshheritage.com/wild-atlantic-way-ireland/ and join us as we slowly travel along the Wild 'Ancestry' Way.

Slán for now, Mike :)

Your Ideal Trip to Ireland

September 7, 2014

Céad Míle Fáilte—and welcome to your 'Letter from Ireland' on another lovely sunny Sunday morning here in Cork (it's beginning to feel like a record!). However, the evenings are closing in and it's dark by about 8.30pm. The heating will need to come on soon.

I'm back on the Barry's tea this morning—and I do hope you'll have a cup of whatever you fancy as you join me for today's Letter.

As I mentioned a moment ago—we're losing daylight either side of the day and it feels like we should hit the road for one or two more road trips before long. And that's the subject of our Letter this morning—taking the ideal trip around Ireland.

What's Your Ideal Trip to Ireland?

Many of the emails I receive each week are concerned with planning a trip to Ireland. Often, it is a first trip—and the person on the other end is worried that they are fitting enough in, going to the right places, etc. You know yourself how enjoyable—and stressful—holiday planning can be!

The main questions I get asked are of the following two flavours:

1. *'It's my first visit to Ireland—should I take a tour bus or rent a*

car? The thought of driving a car in Ireland makes me nervous!'

2. *'I will be staying near Ballyancestry—where my people came from— but I also want to visit The Cliffs of Moher/ Blarney/ Dublin/ Galway—how far away are they?'*

My answer to number one is—yes, you can always take a tour— but you can also mix it up a bit. For example, stay three days in Dublin with no car, take some day trips. Take a small three day tour to some further locations. Then rent a car for another three days and go where you want. No need to play by other people's rules (that wouldn't be very Irish, would it?)

I have found that most people use a guided coach tour the first time around—then come back for second helpings, opting for a car on this second trip. Has this been your experience?

The Ideal 'Recipe' for a Trip to Ireland.

On the second question—well, let's step back a bit first.

Most of the people who read this letter have ancestry linked with Ireland. The places your ancestors came from are often the places you want to visit. Along with these essential places, there are sights and landmarks that you would LOVE to see this time around.

I have found that many of us have ten days or so available for a trip to Ireland. A mistake we can make (and organised tours seem to take this approach) is to hurry from one sight to another, spending barely a night in one spot.

Somehow, I notice that the ideal 'recipe' for a trip to Ireland over ten days/nine nights is to spend 2-3 nights in about three separate locations—and use these as bases for exploration. You can often easily explore within fifty miles of these 'bases'—and also have the flexibility to absorb more of the local colour. Also, it is definitely less hassle than packing up early each morning and heading on. Here are three examples:

The Southwest and Dublin.

Diane wrote to me. Her ancestors came from the Skibbereen area of County Cork, so she wanted to ensure she visited there. But she also wanted to visit Cobh, Dingle and the Cliffs of Moher.

My suggestions were:

1. Use Bantry town as base number one. Skibbereen is about ten miles away. The Beara peninsula is on your doorstep. Kenmare in Kerry is about fifteen miles away. The Mizen Peninsula is on your doorstep. The Ring of Kerry is doable in a day. Cork city is about one-hour drive away and Cobh about twenty five miles beyond that.

2. Use Dingle town as base number two. The Dingle Peninsula is on your doorstep. When travelling from Bantry to Dingle, you could go around the Ring of Kerry.

3. Use Dublin City as base number three. Dublin is Dublin! Good idea to stay local—give back the keys of the car—and take a day tour to Newgrange, Tara or Glendalough.

That's one example of three bases—nine nights.

The Northwest and Dublin.

Kathi also wrote to me. Her ancestry traced back to Sligo town—so she wanted to ensure she visited there.

My suggestions were:

1. Use Sligo town as base number one. The small county of Sligo is on your doorstep. You can drive north to Donegal town, east into Leitrim and Fermanagh, and south into North County Mayo—all on easy day trips.

2. Use Derry City as base number two. It's a beautiful, small and safe city—plenty to see. You can also use it as a springboard into the Inishowen Peninsula of Donegal, east along the north Antrim Coast (maybe a day trip to Belfast at a push) and south into County Tyrone and the Ulster American folk park.

3. Use Dublin City as base number three. As with my previous suggestion of Dublin.

Another example of three bases—nine nights.

The West and Dublin.

George wrote to me. His family was from west of Galway City in County Galway as well as County Mayo.

My suggestions were:

1. Use Galway city as base number one. Hard to leave this historical small city when you arrive—but if you must you could: head off into the wilds of Connemara; visit the Aran Islands for a day; visit the north coast of Clare down to the Cliffs of Moher; head into historical east Galway to the town of Athenry. An alternative would be to stay for two or three nights on Inis Mór—the largest of the Aran Islands. It is an experience that will stay with

you for the rest of your life.

2. Use Westport in County Mayo as base number two. Westport is a gem of a town—plenty going on here. However, when you have to leave you can head south into Connemara or north along the Mayo coast.

3. Use Dublin City as base number three. As with my previous suggestion of Dublin.

A final example of three bases—nine nights.

These are just some of the three-centre holidays I would be happy to go on! But they are personal choices. Now, let me ask you—what would be your ideal three-centre holiday in Ireland if you had ten days/nine nights?

I know we have so much experience of travel in Ireland among our readers—so I will do my best to publish all of your suggestions that come my way. But, be sure to limit it to three-centre holiday suggestions over nine nights.

And that's it for another week!

Slán for now, Mike :)

McCarthy's Bar

October 5, 2014

Céad Míle Fáilte—and welcome to your 'Letter from Ireland' on a changeable Sunday morning here in Cork. First let me say, thank you so much for all your well-wishes last week—I'm well on the mend—and I must say Carina did do a great job with the stories from her own family.

She has now many requests for more stories going into the future!

I'm having a glass of water from the well this morning—back to the simple things in life—and I do hope you'll have a cup of whatever you fancy as you join me for today's Letter.

Have you been on a trip to Ireland?

Last week, Patrick Mullen (one of our Green Room members) was looking for help. You see, he was planning his first trip to Ireland and was concerned about

a) driving on the 'wrong side of the road' and

b) the driving habits of the native Irish!

He was wondering should he go for a bus tour or hire a car with all the uncertainties that might bring! Maybe you've been faced with this decision in the past? Anyway, he got a mountain of suggestions and advice and I'm sure he'll figure out the right thing for himself.

However, I felt that Patrick should also read the following book before making up his mind—'McCarthy's Bar' by Pete McCarthy. Maybe you have read it?

Always Go Into a Bar With Your Name Over the Door.

I'm always struck by the connection most of our readers feel with the land, people and culture of Ireland. Some people call it a 'genetic memory'—others just like to think of it as 'coming home' when they manage to make the trip. Pete McCarthy was second-generation Irish who was born in England to an English father and an Irish mother. He spent many of his early summers with his Irish cousins near the West Cork town of Drimoleague in the 1960s.

He always questioned the attraction he felt to Ireland and his own resulting identity. Was he an English man? An Irish man? In 1999 he made a trip around the west of Ireland. He travelled around a country that was rapidly changing into a modern economy. He was an acute observer with many ties to the country through his own family. He was also a brilliant comic writer! He wandered the land in a Volvo nicknamed 'The Tank' that was on its last legs, and spontaneously made his way from one hilarious encounter to the next.

He had a general plan, but let each day uncover its own possibility. He was also fond of the warmth and conviviality to be found in the pubs of Ireland and had the guiding principle of 'never passing a pub that had my name over the door'. His surname was McCarthy. That involved a lot of pubs in the south of Ireland!

The book McCarthy's Bar was published in 2000 and went on they sell well over a million copies around the world. It is still well worth the buy. Especially if you are planning a trip to Ireland and you need to sprinkle your timetable with healthy doses of inspiration and serendipity.

Aussie Bikers, a Convent and Surreal Encounters.

If you do read the book 'McCarthy's Bar', you'll hear Pete talking about 'Con and Karen' and his favourite lodgings—a wonderful convent turned into a guest house somewhere in West Cork.

Con (which is short for Conn!) and Karen are friends of ours and they used to run this convent guesthouse near Timoleague in West Cork. I'd like to tell you a story they told me about Pete McCarthy.

After Pete stayed at their 'convent' while researching his book in 1999, he became a close friend and returned many times with his family over the years. Over those years, 'McCarthy's Bar' became more famous and attracted many 'pilgrims' to the country to travel in the footsteps of Pete.

One morning, the dining room at the convent was really busy so Pete decided to help with serving breakfast. He went up to a table of Aussie bikers who were on a 'McCarthy's Bar' tour of Ireland. They were spending two weeks tracing the obscure places mentioned throughout the book—including the convent where McCarthy spent so much of his 'downtime'.

They carefully explained all this to their waiter—who was none other than Mr. Pete McCarthy himself, but they were completely unaware of who he was. Pete decided not to say anything, probably aware of the possible heart attacks and brain meltdowns that might ensue from such a surreal moment. I do like picturing that story. It is so typical in Ireland—an everyday surreal turn of events.

And back to our reader, Patrick Mullen—I do hope you have a

chance to read McCarthy's Bar—and get a sense of the treasures that may come your way on this island when you open yourself up to the magic of spontaneous everyday encounters. Take a coach or hire a car? I know which one I'd do. Also, if you head to the right part of the country, you'll find plenty of pubs with 'Mullen' over the door.

That's it for this week.

Slán for now, Mike :)

From Milltown to Milltown

October 12, 2014

Céad Míle Fáilte—and welcome to your Letter from Ireland. It's a beautiful autumn's morning here in Cork. Early morning mists that burn off by about 10:00 am—a really unique time of the year. I hope the weather is at least as nice in your part of the world.

I do hope you are keeping well wherever you are today. I'm back on the Barry's tea this morning and I do hope you'll have a cup of whatever you fancy yourself and join me for today's Letter.

One of our readers—Pádraic Mac Coitir (that translates into McCotter or Cotter in English—a fine Irish Viking name!)—was on to me during the week. Pádraic is a local tour guide in his home county of Antrim and also writes some very nice pieces for his local paper.

So, Pádraic is going to be our guest letter writer this morning with his piece 'Milltown to Milltown'. He has a lovely style in his writing with wonderful observations threaded into the history of the places he walks through. Before you read, I'd also like to explain a couple of references that you will come across in the piece. You will see a reference to 'H-Block'—you see, Pádraic was a political prisoner in the North in the late 1970s. You will also later see a reference to 'Antrim shirts'—meaning the colours of the Antrim GAA football team. As he points out, sections of the loyalist community can choose to see this as a provocative gesture.

As I read this piece it reminded me of how much things have changed in the north of Ireland over the past 10 years—and how hard it is to understand the deep-seated cultural divides that exist unless you live there, like Pádraic.

So, I hope you will enjoy this 'walk with Pádraic'—and the colour and insights he offers into life in parts of the north of Ireland today and in the recent past.

Milltown to Milltown.

Sometimes we tend to think that going on a journey full circle involves a cruise or going from the Glens of Antrim to the hills of Donegal and back again. I've been to Donegal many's the time but still waiting to go on a cruise!

The other day I went on a far shorter, but just as enjoyable, journey from Milltown cemetery to Milltown near Derriaghy and back again. I'd never walked this particular route but my friend Tommy runs it often and assured me that it's 'only a stroll'. So off we went up the Glen Road, past the Glenowen Inn (even though we were tempted to get a bite to eat after the smell of the cooking hit our nostrils) and on to where the brewery is being demolished. It brought back memories of when I worked there on 'summer relief' in 1976 only for that particular job to be cut short when I ended up in Castlereagh and then the H-Blocks for the first of my time in prison.

As we went on up the road we commented on the changes happening with the new housing developments. There's an obvious need for homes so hopefully this will be the start of a new and positive community. St. Theresa's CLG will no doubt benefit from this and perhaps they will take on the mantle of a successful club. Despite the temptation we hurried on past the Roddy's and headed into the country (yes, only a half hour's walk from the bottom of the Glen Road!).

While walking along the Colinwell Road we had to be wary of the traffic, especially the many lorries that passed. I've spoken to Brendan from the Farmer's Inn about this and I'm sure he'd love to see a footpath along this part of the road which no doubt would make it easier for people to get to his pub. The Farmer's Inn is one of the best bars you could visit, especially when Brendan is there to give a brief history of the place in which it's located. On this occasion the mission was still on so no stopping at this water hole!

The Barnfield Road is about a half mile from the bar and once on to it the views can be appreciated as far as the Mountains of Mourne to the right and Strangford Lough to the left. Further down the road is a small church with a graveyard beside it. I never knew this church existed but it's been there a long time. In fact there's a cross above the door which proclaims the church was 'rebuilt' in 1755. Tommy told me someone told him that Oliver Plunkett had worshiped there at one time. Is this the reason for the name of the parish in Lenadoon? Finding places off the beaten track throws these questions up!

So after walking around the cemetery we went on down to Milltown village. Wearing our Antrim tops we were wary walking past the shops which welcome visitors to loyalist Milltown—and just in case one couldn't make out the writing the many flags were there to remind us that bigotry is alive and well. The last time I'd been there the village pub had a thatched roof and it was always a place I'd love to have had a pint in, but again the number of loyalist flags put me off. The pub had a sign pointing out that it was built in the 17th century. This area is obviously steeped in history and as a political tour guide I'd love to find out more about it.

Our final destination was the local church and its graveyard. Going through the main gates—its clear the place is very well maintained with the graves clean and the gardens full of flowers. One of the first graves we saw was that of the Duffin family. Being interested in our political past we noticed that there was reference to a William Gould Duffin who died of gunshot wounds on the 15th February 1922. There was nothing to indicate how William met his fate so I said to Tommy I'll check it out when we got home. We spent a bit of time in the church grounds checking out other interesting graves but I wanted to find out more about William Duffin—we walked on down the road to the library in Dairy Farm but the internet didn't have any information.

When I got home I went into the index of Jim McDermott's book, 'Northern Divisions' and saw a reference to William Duffin. He was working as an apprentice manager at his father's spinning mill in Northumberland Street when a number of IRA men approached and killed him. No one knows for sure why he was shot but Jim asserts in his book that it may have been because his brother was a member of the 'Northern Ireland Senate'. William lived a short distance from where Tommy and I started our walk—Roselands on the Andersonstown Road.

Thanks for that 'letter' this week, Pádraic!

Slán for now, Mike :)

Section 3: The Irish Diaspora

A River and an Irish Surname

March 23, 2014

Céad Míle Fáilte from County Cork—and I trust you are doing well wherever you are in the world as you read this. We seem to be in the middle of 'four seasons in one day' type of weather here at the moment—hard to get out without getting wet but too nice to be staying in. Well, at least the slugs are enjoying the weather! I'm sitting down with a nice pick-me-up cup of coffee this morning (I was at a 50th birthday last night), so why don't you have a cup of whatever you fancy and join me for today's Letter?

A River and an Irish Surname.

I was watching the telly the other night and a lovely programme called 'Abhainn' came on. It features a different Irish river (Abhainn is the Irish for river—pronounced 'oww-an') each week and brings us on a trip from source to sea over a half hour. This week it was the turn of the River Bandon in County Cork.

The River Bandon gets its name from the Celtic goddess for water—Bann—and rises near the town of Drimoleague. Through the many aerial shots used in the programme we see all the towns, bridges and castles along the way. And we meet many of the local characters. During its first few miles, the river flows through country associated with the O'Donovan family name. A few months back I travelled around this area and came across one of the castles shown in the programme—Togher Castle—a stronghold of the McCarthys.

As I stood there taking pictures from a distance on a cloudy day, a man came out of a nearby farmhouse. We nodded and stood beside each other looking at the castle in the distance. It turned out that he bought the castle with the farm a few years back.

He was a Donovan who had been on the road all his life while running a transport company. He decided to settle down twenty years ago and bought the farm—and now he told me that 'the only way I'll be out of here is in the foxy box'. We talked a while about the castle and its history—and how we might be related (I'm part Donovan also)—and after a while we parted.

It resonated with me how this man had made a decision about the place he wanted to stay and see out his days. I suppose for a lot of us it is a privilege to be able to choose your final resting place.

Then, a few days later I saw a mail from one of our readers, Melinda Stahl. A story about another Donovan and how he got to choose his final resting place.

A Lake and an Irish Surname.

Melinda's story was about the Big Rideau Lake in Ontario, Canada—and one of her ancestors:

'My great great great grandfather is Denis Donovan who was born in 1795 in County Cork. By the 1820s he had moved to New York, USA and then

on to Ontario, Canada. In 1842, he bought 50 acres of land in the area near Donovan's Point on the Big Rideau Lake. He and his family operated an apple orchard and market garden in this location. He died on December 18, 1851 and was buried on his property. When his widow and son sold the property in 1860, it was for the entire 50 acres with the exception of a small parcel, 9 feet long by 6 feet wide, and the burial place of Dennis Donovan.

One story (not verified) goes that the deed for this 9 foot by 6 foot wide plot was given to the City of Cork in Ireland. These are the roots of the fictional 'Rideau Canal worker buried in Irish soil' story that appeared in local newspapers. Donovan's headstone was found in 1970, it read 'DENIS DONOVAN departed this life Dec. 18, 1851 aged 56 years, a native of the County Cork, Ireland.'

Thank you very much Melinda for sharing. What a great story! A man who was determined to be buried on Irish-owned soil—and he somehow got his wish. My next step is to head into the archives department in the City Library here in Cork and see if there is any chance of finding such a document that was given by the Donovan family all those years ago. If I find anything—I will let you know.

Do you have any stories about the ancestors in your family?

That's it for now! Slán, Mike... talk next week! :)

Connecting with Your Irish Cousins

July 13, 2014

Céad Míle Fáilte from County Kerry this morning—I'm writing to you from a place known as the 'Homestead of the Rocks'—or Ballinskelligs as it is more usually known. The 'rocks' in question are the wonderful and unique Skellig Rocks off the coast of County Kerry. Maybe you've been here?

Looking out the window of my hostel—I can see Ballinskelligs Priory just ahead of the sea. This was the priory that the monks on Skellig Michael occupied once they finally abandoned their beehive huts in the 1100s.

Amazing to have so many layers of history open out before your eyes!

We're 'doing' the Ring of Kerry on the Wild Atlantic Way at the moment—travelling from Kenmare to Sneem to Caherdaniel to Waterville to Ballinskelligs to Valentia to Cahirciveen to Glenbeigh to Killorglin (phew!)—and I look forward to sharing pictures and more on a blog post later this week.

I'm sitting here with a cup of Lyons tea—why don't you have a cup of whatever you fancy and join me for today's letter?

Connecting With Your Irish Cousins.

As we drive around the Ring of Kerry we come across so many tour buses (it's that time of year!). We stop in the same places, hear mostly American accents and have a chat or two. It becomes clear that many people are here not just for the wonderful scenery—but hope to feel a stronger connection to the places, sounds and people that surrounded their ancestors. We also come across independent travellers who are on hopeful missions to connect with living cousins, uncover forgotten homesteads or to uncover the solid evidence of ancestral headstones in half-forgotten graveyards.

I am sure that someone wise once said 'what makes us human is the need to connect'.

These chats remind me of so many online conversations from the past year. There have been so many great questions, stories and anecdotes. However, given that I live in Ireland—there is one particular flavour of question I hear quite a lot. Let me explain a little more.

Over in our member's forum—The Green Room—we aim to help our readers to solve connection problems in a practical manner. I have noticed that a certain type of conversation comes up from time to time (maybe it's familiar to you too?).

Here is a question from one of our members—he talked about his aim to connect with living Irish cousins:

'I am also aware of the fact that not every person (Irish or otherwise) is keen on being excited that they are related to someone outside of their country, let

alone to be contacted or even visited by such a relative. My point is, I would be ecstatic to reach a relation in Ireland, but I wouldn't want to come to be seen as that creepy cousin that invites himself to family functions and thrusts his company into the lives of those who previously didn't know he existed.

A very good friend of mine, who embraces his Italian heritage, recently had a holiday in Rome. There, after brief conversation with some locals, he was essentially welcomed as a long lost brother, immediately welcomed into the arms of Italy. Would just such a situation be seen as such a big deal in Ireland?'

What a good question! Here is how I answered:

I think you are touching on something that is very obvious to all who attempt to reconnect with their Irish cousins—and it gives good reason to understand the Irish psyche a little better. I recently read the following in a Lonely Planet Ireland guide on Etiquette:

'Conversation is generally friendly but often reserved; the Irish avoid conversations that might embarrass. They are deeply mistrustful of over sharers.'

I think a lot of Irish people would nod when they hear that. It is a good rule of thumb for those from North America to pretend that the Irish they meet are about a generation older than they look.

On the other hand—it is hardwired into our DNA to be as friendly and welcoming as possible. In Brehon Law (Ireland's ancient laws)—one of the most grievous offences (with serious consequences on your honour) was to offer an inappropriate level of welcome and shelter to those who requested it. This surface (and genuine) friendliness—yet simultaneous reservation can be confusing to some.

Everybody's experience is different—but I think it is always good to persist with an open mind, a welcoming heart, no preconceptions and no expectation! Who knows what wonderful—and unexpected—connections you may make!

What about you? I'd love to hear your stories and insights. What are your hopes and experiences in connecting with your Irish 'cousins'?

That's it for now!

Slán, Mike... talk next week! :)

What Part of the Irish Diaspora Do You Come From?

July 27, 2014

Céad Míle Fáilte—and I hope you are keeping well on what is a lovely summer morning here in County Cork. Everyone seems to be heading away on their 'holliers' (as we say in Cork) in these parts—and we are due to head off on our holidays this week to the wonderful Dingle Peninsula in County Kerry.

I'm having a cup of Lyons tea this morning—and I do hope you'll have a cup of whatever you fancy, sit back and join me for this morning's Letter.

Which Part of the Irish Diaspora Do You Come From?

Don't you just love the word 'Diaspora'? Apparently, it comes from the Greek word for 'scattering'. The reason I bring this up today is because Ireland has appointed its very first 'Minister for the Diaspora'—Jimmy Deenihan.

I first remember the word being used in the context of an 'Irish Diaspora' when President Mary Robinson used to light a candle of welcome each night in all the windows of the presidential residence. A symbol of guidance and welcome for people of Irish descent spread throughout the world.

Now there are about 80 million people around the world who claim significant Irish descent. Quite amazing for such a small country as ours!

The following is a rough breakdown of where we find our Irish today:

- **USA:** About 36 million people identify themselves as primarily of Irish descent. One of the things that surprised me when I started 'A Letter from Ireland' was just how many readers we have of Scotch-Irish descent (and that is a subject coming soon in the Letter)—about 20% of all our readers.

- **Canada:** About 4.5 million of Irish descent. Most Irish headed to Canada from the 19th century famine all the way to the 1950s. Even today, Canadian companies turn up in Ireland each year in quantity to recruit whole families of skilled tradesmen to all sorts of infrastructure and mining projects across the country.

- **South American countries**: Claim high Irish descent populations—2.5% in Argentina and 3.6% in Uruguay. The majority of these are descendants of the families of soldiers who first left Ireland as 'Wild Geese' to fight with the Spanish armies—and followed them onto the colonies. People like Bernardo O'Higgins—the founder of the Argentinian Navy.

- **Australia**: Just over 10% of the Australian population self-declare as being of Irish ancestry. I am always struck by the stories that come from our Australian readers.

52

Many of their ancestors arrived in the colony as convicted criminals—and the story around their conviction was often captured in court proceedings back in Ireland. And harrowing stories they are too.

- **Great Britain**: About 10% of its population is of Irish descent. Our US readers often question how Irish people could go and live in Britain. The answer is simple—job prospects and it was often where their family and friends already resided. My own parents moved to Britain. I was born there. We all moved back to Ireland. I went back to work there for a short while. My own son now works there. That is the way it has been for many centuries.

So, if you were passing on advice to our new Minister for the Diaspora—Jimmy Deenihan—what would you say? What questions would you have for him?

In the meantime, thank you so much for being a part of the 'Letter from Ireland' community—I think we have become a living example of just how people of Irish descent around the world can connect together.

That's it for now!

Slán, Mike... talk next week! :)

The First Citizen of Canada

August 3, 2014

Céad Míle Fáilte—and I hope you are keeping well on what is a sunny morning here in Cork. Although August marks the official beginning of autumn—in Ireland we like to think of summer lasting until the final day of August. We take what we can!

We're just back from a trip to the lovely Dingle peninsula as part of our tour around the Wild Atlantic Way—and this week we start the next leg from Tralee in County Kerry all the way up to Doolin in County Clare. Maybe you've been to some of these places?

I'm back on the Barry's tea as we speak—and I do hope you'll have a cup of whatever you enjoy and join me for this morning's 'Letter from Ireland'.

Is This the Story of Your Irish Ancestor?

In last week's Letter from Ireland, we talked about the 'Irish Diaspora' and I asked what part of the diaspora you came from. Well—the response was second to none (that's very good in Irish parlance!). I spent until last Thursday reading replies that traced the tracks of many of your Irish ancestors. So many questions—so many unexpected twists and turns—and a fair share of sadness too.

What struck me was how so many traits of the Irish character shone through in the stories. Perhaps that was because so many of these people were thrown into situations where they had little choice but to plow ahead and make good of whatever turned up on their path.

This week, I'd like to feature just one of these stories. This is the story of one reader's ancestor, Louis Aubry, who became the first recorded Irish-born settler in what is now modern Canada.

Have a read and see if it reminds you of the story of your ancestors.....

The First Irish-Born Settler in Canada.

In the 2006 census—about 4.4 million people in Canada described themselves as being of Irish origin. 350 years earlier, in 1663, the first census was held in the outpost of Ville Marie (modern-day Montreal). It listed 3,035 residents.

Among them was a man who became known as Pierre Aubry. However, his name on arrival in Ville Marie was not Pierre Aubry—it was Tadhg Cornelius O'Brennan. And Tadhg was the first recorded settler in the territories that later made up the modern state of Canada.

So, what brought Tadhg to this part of the world a full 200 years before many of his Irish Catholic neighbours?

Tadhg came from the O'Brennan families of north Kilkenny. As we discussed in The Tribes of Ireland book—they came from the old Irish tribal lands known as the Osraighe (Ossary) which covered most of modern County Kilkenny and part of south County Laois.

The chief family of the area were the Fitzpatricks—but many 'Tuatha' (small kingdoms) were governed by families such as the O'Brennans for hundreds of years. However, by 1652, Oliver Cromwell had swept through the island in a brutal campaign which culminated in the 'Act of Settlement'. This piece of legislation effectively confiscated the majority of Irish Catholic-owned land. Among the land affected was that belonging to the O'Brennans previously for hundreds of years.

The displaced Irish were given the choice to go 'To Hell or to Connaught'—although many ended up as slaves in the West Indies—and over 30,000 ended up as soldiers in the armies of France and Spain, becoming the 'Wild Geese' that we know today. Tadhg O'Brennan was one of those who chose to join the armies of France at the age of twenty. He moved to the Celtic region of Brittany in Northwest France, and this was one of the regions to supply soldiers and planters to the new colonies in North America.

Tadhg turns up near modern Montreal—in what was known as Ville Marie—for the first time in 1661. He is recorded as being in the employ of a local farmer, and we hear of him only because he was one of a number kidnapped by a band of Iroquois. He remained a captive from March to October and was one of the lucky few to escape with their lives. By the Ville Marie census of 1663, Tadhg had become known as 'Thecle Cornelius Aubrenan'.

The same census recorded that while there were 1,293 single men in Ville Marie—Tadhg among them—there were only nine single women of child-bearing age. This prompted King Louis XIV of France to send on 'les filles du Roi' (daughters of the King) to help the situation out a little. These 'daughters' consisted of 770 women who arrived in the new colony between 1663 and 1673. In fact, more than 95 per cent of French-Canadians can trace their ancestors to women in that group. Naturally, this group also caught the attention of Tadhg.

Tadhg tried hard for seven years to win himself a bride from each new boat arrival of 'les Filles du Roi'—but eventually realised that he needed to head downriver to Quebec City, where the first women disembarked, to increase his odds of success. This he did— and on July 31, he met Jeanne Chartier. Tadhg and Jeanne were married September 10, 1670.

The newlyweds settled in what is now the island of Montreal, and had seven children—three girls and four boys. Four of the children died before the age of five. The last two girls, born in 1679 and 1681, died soon after birth. Tadhg retired at the age of 51 and died four years later, in November 1687.

He was buried in Pointe-Aux-Trembles under the name of Pierre Aubry and was survived by Jeanne and three of their children. We can guess that Tadhg lived a hard and uncertain life—far from all the familiar culture and people he knew so intimately up to the age of 20. He did what he could to survive and push ahead.

Louis Aubry, who kindly shared this story, and the documents related to his ancestor Tadhg, points out that he now has 5,600 descendants of Tadhg on his database living in North America.

And I guess few realise that while many bear the surname Aubrey—they are descended from a man with one of the more common names in the north of County Kilkenny.

Does this sound like the story of your Irish ancestor? The story of Tadhg Cornelius O'Brennan—the first recorded settler in what was to become modern-day Canada.

That's it for now!

Slán, Mike... talk next week! :)

The Scottish Vote for Independence

September 15, 2014

Céad Míle Fáilte—and welcome to your Letter from Ireland on a lovely sunny Sunday morning on the promenade in Salthill, just outside Galway City. Maybe you have been here? We are doing another leg on our journey around Ireland's Wild Atlantic Way—this time travelling from Kilkee in County Clare all the way up to Westport in County Mayo.

Hard work—but someone has to do it!

I'm having a very nice cup of tea and some brown bread in a coffee shop looking out on Galway Bay as I write this—and I do hope you'll have a cup of whatever you fancy as you join me for today's Letter. Although I may be on the west coast of Ireland this morning—and you may be enjoying your own day at home—this week we are going to talk about something a little out of the ordinary, but I feel it is much related to all of our Irish heritage.

You see, a couple of days ago I was having lunch with one Ian Armstrong (Ian designed the cover of my first Letter from Ireland book). His family has been in Cork for generations—but his ancestors came to Cork from County Antrim in Ulster—and before that they arrived in Ireland from the Scottish border counties in the

1600s.

They came to Ireland while Scotland was still an independent kingdom—and many of his Scottish cousins will make an important and related decision this week.

A Scottish Vote for Independence.

When was the last time you remember a country voting for its independence? It's not really an everyday occurrence. However, this Thursday the people of Scotland go to the polls to answer a simple question: 'Should Scotland be an independent country? Yes or No.'

If you were living in Scotland, which way would you vote?

Many of our readers either live in Scotland or have mixed Irish/Scottish ancestry. The readers who live in Scotland typically arrived there as part of migrations following the Great Famine and in subsequent years. They typically came from places like County Donegal and Tyrone.

Also, around 25% of our readers are of 'Scotch-Irish' (or Ulster-Scots) heritage. Their ancestors arrived in Ulster from Scotland—settled for enough generations to consider themselves Irish—and then moved on to the colonies of North America.

As a result, I get many reader questions along the lines of 'Is my name Irish or Scottish?' or 'Is Scots Gaelic the same as Irish Gaelic' and so on.

Scotland Unites for the First Time.

Let's look back a little in time—all the way back—more than one thousand years ago. At the time, much of the land we know as

Scotland was called 'Alba'. The Romans gave a name to the Irish Dál Riada who occupied much of the western coast—they called them the 'Scotti'. This was, in fact, the name that the Romans gave to the Irish.

By the 800s, the Gaelic-speaking Scotti of the West and the Picts of the East came together to form a single kingdom to counter the threat of the Vikings. This united kingdom eventually became known as Scotland—or 'land of the Scotti'.

The Kingdoms of Scotland and England existed side by side for many centuries—hesitant partners and often enemies. In the early 1600s, James the VI of Scotland inherited the throne of England also. This was the first time that a single king held both thrones at once. His coronation helped to usher in a period of stability—especially around the border areas where raiding families made it a very dangerous place for traveling. Raiding families like the Armstrongs mentioned at the start of this letter.

At the same time, King James had tremendous problems with the 'wildest' part of the Kingdom of Ireland—around the counties of Ulster. This prompted the first of the main 'plantations' from Scotland and border areas to Ireland. Perhaps James thought he was settling two problems at once!

As the 1600s moved on, more planters moved from the lowlands of Scotland and the border regions to the counties of Ulster. They were mostly Presbyterian—which was considered a wayward religion (with no respect for hierarchy) by the establishment.

But towards the end of the 1600s, Scotland was becoming a much poorer place in comparison to neighbouring England, which was feasting on the riches of its new colonies. Also, Scotland's mainly Presbyterian population suffered a high degree of religious persecution while a famine towards the end of the century wiped out about 20% of the population. These events drove high emigration numbers both from Scotland to Ireland, as well as directly to the North American colonies (Ireland was also seen as a colony for much of the 1600s).

Things were getting desperate.

Scotland Loses its Independence For the First Time.

In the 1690s, a number of moneyed Scots saw an opportunity to establish Scotland's first colony. They called it Caledonia and it was located where the Panama Canal is today. Much excitement was generated and the scheme was heavily funded for success. However, due to political manoeuvring by competitors such as the East India Company, bad planning and bad luck, the scheme was a failure.

In fact, it was a disaster. Up to 30% of all the money circulating in Scotland was lost in this debacle. This left many figures of the Scottish establishment hurting and in need of support (and many of them were members of Scotland's parliament).

In stepped England with a possible solution. England was compromised militarily and Scotland was a weak neighbour to the north. Negotiations began for the uniting of the Kingdoms of Scotland and England.

These negotiations completed in 1706 and Scotland received a guarantee of access to the colonies for trade. Members of the Scottish establishment who lost so much in their Panama investment were compensated (and many of these people were also the negotiators). England had won a reliable ally and Scotland had won an economic future.

The treaty was hugely unpopular in Scotland. It was noted that it was 'contrary to the inclinations of at least three-fourths of the Kingdom'. There were many threats of rioting and martial law was imposed.

On May 1st, 1707, the United Kingdom of England and Scotland came into being.

Remember my friend Ian Armstrong from the top of this article? Well, by this time, his ancestors and those of many of our Ulster-Scots readers had departed for Ireland as well as directly to the North American colonies. Meanwhile, the ancestors of our readers who live today in Scotland had yet to arrive from Ireland!

It took at least thirty years for Scotland to benefit from access to the colonies of the United Kingdom. By the 1760s, Glasgow was the major world centre for tobacco importing and shipbuilding.

And so, Scotland has remained part of the United Kingdom to this day. The last country to leave this United Kingdom was most of the island of Ireland, which in 1922, won independence and later became the Republic of Ireland. But it took until the 1960s for real prosperity to hit Irish shores for the first time. At the time, Ireland certainly did not seek its independence for economic reasons. I wonder which way Ian Armstrong's cousins will vote this Thursday?

Do you have Scottish ancestors? Which way do you think they would have voted?

That's it for now.

Slán for now, Mike :)

Note: On September 18th, 2014—the people of Scotland voted to remain part of the United Kingdom by a small majority.

Was Your Ancestor on this First Great Migration?

November 3, 2014

Céad Míle Fáilte—and welcome to your Letter from Ireland. We've just come out the other end of a 'soft' week (in Ireland, 'soft' is often used as a replacement word for 'wet'). Things are brightening up for the morning here in Cork and we might even get out and about a little later to take a few photos.

I'm having a nice cup of Lyon's tea as I write, so I do hope you'll join me now with a cup of whatever you fancy yourself as we settle into today's Letter from Ireland.

Do you own a piece of linen? How about Irish Linen? Maybe a nice tablecloth or even a cool dress or nice shirt? A few weeks back, I received this email from Joan Adams:

'My ancestor, William Irwin, was born in County Antrim about 1703 and immigrated about 1741. I have long wanted to find out more about him, but I don't really know where to start.'

The date of 1741 caught my attention immediately. You see, that was a very difficult year for everyone on the island of Ireland.

Ulster Linen and the Start of a Great Migration.

Flax was grown in Ireland, and linen was woven from this flax, for many centuries. However, the quality and sizing of this linen meant it was never in demand from the larger markets across the UK and Europe. From the middle of the 1600s, the 'Plantation of Ulster' was in full flight. Tenant farmers were enticed from Scotland and the border counties of England to land taken from the native Irish across the Ulster counties of Antrim, Down, Armagh, Derry, Monaghan, Cavan, Tyrone and Donegal.

These immigrants brought with them a skillset that was capable of manufacturing linen suitable for sale across the markets of Europe. The majority of these weavers and farmers put parts of their farms aside for the growing of flax. By the early 1700s, Huguenots were offered freedom from religious persecution on the continent and brought more sophisticated weaving and manufacturing techniques to their new homes in Ulster.

Shortly after, the weaving of linen became the main export activity of Counties Antrim, Armagh, Down, Monaghan, Derry, Tyrone and Cavan—and accounted for 25% of all exports from Ireland.

While the flax used for manufacturing linen was grown across Ulster, the seed used for the flax was imported from the Baltic States up to the early 1700s. Then, in 1731, the colonies of North America were permitted to export flaxseed back to Ireland and the United Kingdom for the first time.

This seed from the colonies was in high demand across the farms of Ulster. Also, as the population of the colonies increased, so too did their demand for fine linen from the weavers of Ireland. As a result, ships arrived from the colonies (particularly from Pennsylvania) to the ports of Derry, Newry, Belfast and Coleraine loaded up with flaxseed for feeding into the local linen industry. They then stocked up with a return boatload of fine linen for the growing markets in the colonies.

However, the ships were taking a smaller return load of this fine and light linen—and the owners looked around for additional cargo to take to the colonies on their sparsely-loaded ships. The answer was people—new emigrants from the north of Ireland to the colonies. The shipping companies went into strong competition with each other to entice the tenant farmers of Ulster to leave their homes of several generations and strike off for a new life in the colonies of North America.

But, why would these (mainly Protestant) farmers want to leave their established homes in the province of Ulster for such an uncertain future?

An Untold Story—The Famine of 1741.

A combination of factors gave them motive to emigrate to the colonies with the risk of losing so much. Many of the original 'planters' from the north of England and Scotland were attracted to Ulster by the promise of fertile lands and steady rents. They were tenant farmers on land that was owned by the larger (and mostly absent) English and Scottish lords. As the population and economic stability of Ulster increased, it was accompanied by a steady increase of rents (what became known as 'rent-racking').

A second factor made it nearly impossible to pay these increasing rents. Nowadays, our history tells us mostly of the Great Irish Famine of the 1840s. However, the years between 1726 and 1741 brought a number of droughts and frosts—with resulting food shortages that hit famine levels. In 1741 alone, about 20% of the population of the island of Ireland died through famine and related sickness.

1741 was the year that Joan Adam's ancestor—William Irwin— left his life in Ulster for the colonies of North America. He must have left a very harsh life behind him that year.

By 1775, about 200,000 men and women from the counties of Ulster had migrated to the colonies of North America. About half of these were indentured servants and the majority were Presbyterian of Scottish ancestry. When they arrived they were simply known as Irish—that is how they saw themselves—and later became labelled as 'Scotch-Irish'.

Their colonial attitude and skills made them suitable for living on frontiers of the colonies—western Pennsylvania, the Carolinas and on to Kentucky and Tennessee, where you will still find their descendants today. This great migration from Ulster to the colonies came to an abrupt end in 1776 with the American Revolution.

When I started the Letter from Ireland—and began a conversation with so many of our readers, I was surprised to find that as many as 20% of all of our readers were descendants of these 'Ulster-Scots'. Men and women who left the counties of Ulster through the 1700s for a new life in the colonies of North America.

Readers like Joan Adams who asked her question about William Irving at the top of the letter.

Do you have an Ulster-Scot ancestor in your family tree?

That's it for this week—as always, do feel free to comment below. Thank you again for being a part of the Letter from Ireland.

Slán for now, Mike and Carina :)

Did Your Ancestor follow the 'Black Velvet Band'?

Céad Míle Fáilte—and welcome to your Letter from Ireland. The weather is behaving quite well here in Cork at the moment. It's dark by 5.30pm at this time of year but we are having some nice bright days. I hope the weather is staying nice and clement wherever you are today.

I'm settling into a nice cup of Barry's tea, so I do hope you'll join me now with a cup of whatever you fancy yourself—and we'll start into today's Letter from Ireland.

Last week, Maggie Heffernan of New South Wales in Australia sent the following note:

'Heffernan is my married name and our first Heffernan in Australia was William who was sent out to Australia for 7 years for committing perjury in 1848, he was an 'exile'—a more politically correct term for convict! William arrived on the same ship as 2 John Heffernan's, a father & son who were convicted of sheep stealing, I am in contact with a descendant of these two men and to this day we cannot connect the two families.

I hope some of the above information may be of interest and maybe some of your members may be able to help me in finding out more of my Irish heritage. Regards, Maggie Heffernan.'

Maggie is just one of the 2.1 Million Australian citizens who identified themselves as being of Irish ancestry in the 2011 census. When I hear from our Australian readers, there is often at least one story of 'transportation to a penal colony' in their ancestry. These stories are often colourful, unjust and well-recorded in the record books. We have lots of songs that capture the sentiment and hardship of many of these forced transportations. Songs like 'The Black Velvet Band' which was made popular by the Dubliners.

Maybe you know these lines?

'Before judge and jury next morning
Both of us did appear
A gentleman claimed his jewellery
And the case against us was clear

Now seven long years transportation
Right down to Van Diemen's land
Far away from my friends and companions
To follow the black velvet band'

But, before we have a look at Ireland and Australia at the time of William Heffernan, let's look at the surname Heffernan itself.

The Four Tribes of Owney.

Maggie's Irish surname—Heffernan—is one of those names that did not change much with anglicisation. It comes from the Irish 'Ó hIfernáin' which derives in turn from the first name 'Ifernan'. This is a descriptive first name—and a rather fierce one—which loosely translates as 'small demon from hell'. A useful description when you want your reputation to ride before you in more war-like times!

The Ó hIfernáin family came out of what is now County Clare, around the village of Corofin. One branch of the family headed east to an area in modern county Tipperary that became known as Owney. There, they established themselves as one of the main families of the area—becoming one of the 'Four Tribes of Owney'—alongside the Lynch, McKeogh and Callahan families.

Over time, they in turn were displaced by the Mulryans—but the family name is still located to this day in the east of County Limerick, west Tipperary and the original homeland in County Clare. Maggie's ancestor William, who left from Tipperary—was probably connected alright to his fellow Heffernan passengers, but that relationship may have been from centuries in the past.

I'm also sure that many more Heffernans left this part of Ireland for Australia over the years 1791 to 1853.

Seven Long Years Transportation.

With the end of the American War of Independence, Britain needed a new destination for the convicts that were selected for transportation. The colony of New South Wales (which included much of modern Queensland) was selected as a good alternative. Legislation was put into place in 1786 that allowed Irish courts to choose transportation to N.S.W. as a sentencing choice.

The first Irish convict ship left for N.S.W. in April of 1791 and between 1791 and 1853, approximately 30,000 Irish people were transported to N.S.W. The last ship to carry convicts left Kingstown, near Dublin, and arrived in Australia on the 30th of August, 1853.

Of course, it wasn't just Ireland that provided Australia with her convict labour over all of this time, about 165,000 convicts were transported from England, Scotland and Ireland combined.

However, much has been made of the trivial offences that could get you into trouble in the Irish courts—and there seems to be some truth in this. One observer noted that English law in Ireland seemed to be the most severe across the United Kingdom for minor crimes:

'A man is vanished from Scotland for a great crime, from England for a small on, and from Ireland, for hardly no crime at all.'

The Irish were sent almost exclusively to New South Wales and by 1837 about 30% of the N.S.W. population was Irish and Catholic. The vast majority of these were convicts, freed convicts or the children of freed convicts.

This flow of convicts to the colonies was a much-needed source of labour in a land without infrastructure and cultivation. From the beginning of the transportation system, a convict arrived in N.S.W. and was assigned to a specific farm owner—the more dangerous prisoners were sent directly to work on road gangs. Seven years was the typical duration of a sentence, but of course many did not have the option of returning to their homeland at the end of that period. Also, a system of 'probation' was in place, which allowed a man to be eligible for conditional freedom after 4 years for good behaviour.

The typical Irish man who arrived in N.S.W. was from a farm labouring background back in Ireland. He rarely had a trade or marketable skill. On release, it was going to be through the hard work of farming that he established himself in his adopted country. The trend emerged that Irish convicts, once obtaining freedom, took up land grants all over N.S.W., Queensland and the other newly established Australian States.

I'll finish with a note I received from our good friend Des Dineen (who loves in Melbourne, Australia). He pointed out that

'...a large proportion of Irish migrants to Australia in the mid-1800s came from Tipperary, generally from a 40 mile radius of the Rock of Cashel.'

That was news to me—and very interesting—as it brings us full circle to Maggie Heffernan's opening letter about her ancestor. It appears that William Heffernan was one of the many Tipperary residents who were forcibly removed from their homeland hundreds of years ago—and somehow survived and thrived in the land that Maggie and her family are proud to call home today.

Was your ancestor transported to the colonies? What was their story?

That's it for this week—as always, do feel free to reply and say hello, share an Irish surname or story in your family. Thank you again for being a part of the Letter from Ireland.

Slán for now—Mike and Carina :)

Section 4: Culture, Customs, Music and Craic

It's a Long Way to Tipperary

June 1, 2014

Céad Míle Fáilte from County Cork—and I hope you are doing well wherever you might be in the world this morning. It's the first of June as I write—the real start of summer in Ireland.

I just realised that this is number 53 of the weekly Letter from Ireland—which means that it is one year and one week ago today that I first sat down to write and wondered 'will anyone ever be interested in this letter?'

Well, I need never have worried—along the way I've picked up such an engaged and lovely group of people of Irish ancestry from all over the world! So, thank you for being here and taking the time to join me each Sunday morning!

It's Barry's tea for me this morning, so why don't you have a cup of whatever you fancy and join me for today's 'Letter from Ireland'?

It's a Long Way to Tipperary.

Now, you've probably heard of Tipperary—in fact you may know it very well! The old World War I tune 'It's a Long Way to Tipperary' was originally 'It's a Long Way to Connemara' (that will be a different letter!). It was co-written by one Jack Judge whose grandparents came from Tipperary and I guess it sounded like it WAS a long way away with a name like that. Tipperary is one of the most intriguing counties in Ireland for me.

When the Normans came over in the late 12th century, Tipperary's beautiful vales were a primary target for colonisation and they worked hard to overcome the local Irish chieftains. As a result, alongside the lovely mountain and lake scenery you will find many fine castles and tower-houses dotting Tipperary's landscape.

But now we're going to join Jack Judge, the co-author of 'It's a Long Way to Tipperary' and take a little detour to explore his Irish heritage. Are you ready?

Judges, Brehons and Irish Surnames.

Jack Judge's parents came from County Mayo originally. The surname Judge is an interesting Irish name as it comes from the Irish Mac an Bhreitheamhnaigh (pronounced Mock on vreh-ev-nig) which means 'son of the judge/brehon' in Irish. It is more normally anglicised as 'Breheny' and found in Counties Sligo and Mayo— Jack's parents' home place. I've written before on this Letter about Ireland's Brehon Laws and the Judges, or Brehons, who used to interpret and administer the laws.

The Brehons were a highly trained elite in ancient Ireland. Whole generations of certain families specialised in learning the Brehon Laws. They travelled freely through the kingdoms of Ireland and were typically wealthy as they received a share of the fines settled on following a dispute.

The Brehon Laws were alive and thriving across much of Ireland right up until the mid-17th century when they were replaced by the English Common Law which was developed to serve a more central administrative system. More's the pity that we don't have the many humane aspects of the Brehon Laws with us today! So, old Jack Judge most likely had one (or more) of these Brehons in his Irish ancestry.

Back to Tipperary with the Egans.

One of the more prominent Brehon families was the MacEgans—now normally called Egan (and sometimes Keegan). They travelled from Westmeath to north Tipperary in the 1300s and established a school for the training of Brehons near Lorrha—at what was Redwood or Egan Castle.

It was a powerhouse of Brehon learning over the subsequent centuries—but was eventually destroyed, like so much else in Ireland, by Cromwell's forces in the mid 1600s.

But here is the part I like—and a link back to old Jack Judge's roots in Counties Mayo and Sligo. You see, in 1972 a County Mayo lawyer (by the name of Michael Egan no less)—bought and renovated the castle, bringing it back to a beautiful state and it has been the site of a number of Egan clan gatherings over the past few years. Wouldn't it be nice if we saw more of that sort of family engagement in restoring the buildings and traditions in Ireland?

What do you think?

I think Jack Judge would have approved.

That's it for now! Slán, Mike... talk next week! :)

Meitheamh

June 22, 2014

Céad Míle Fáilte from County Cork —and here we are in the middle of the month of June. We are just past the longest day of the year here in Ireland. Last night didn't seem to happen at all as it stayed bright enough until about 11:00 p.m.

I'm sitting here with a cup of Barry's tea in my hand—why don't you have a cup of whatever you fancy and join me for today's 'Letter from Ireland'?

Meitheamh.

Meitheamh—pronounced 'meh-hev'—is the Irish word for June and more or less means mid-summer. The growth in the fields is at its green height—grass seems to be shooting up an inch a day up to this point.

In the old Celtic Calendar there were four minor festivals through the year on the two solstices and the two equinoxes. Four major festivals then lay between them. Each of these eight festivals had special significance in what was a pastoral society—the fertility and yield of the land had a direct effect on how hungry or how powerful your kingdom would be for the forthcoming year.

Brehon Law dictated that all people would stop work for these festivals and gather in a place overseen by the local king to celebrate. In fact, it was also forbidden to fight during the celebrations and offenders were dealt with very harshly. Now you know why we Irish like to have a good time—it was required by law—and we do like to be good law-abiding citizens!

The mid-summer solstice festival was one of fire—and celebrated on June 23/24. In later years it became known as Saint John's Eve (also Bonfire Night!). Here in Cork there was always a tradition of bonfires on the evening of June 23rd—youngsters would gather old wood and anything that would burn over the weeks leading up to the day. The fire is then lit at a place in the centre of a community, with different smaller traditions in each locality. Sometimes, the ashes are gathered and brought back to vegetable beds and fields to ensure a good harvest.

The other significant happening at this time is the arrival of the first early potatoes. Carina and myself have often sat around a fire—taken potatoes that were dug earlier that day for the first time—wrapped them up and buried them to cook in the embers of the fire. And the taste? Well, there is nothing like that first taste of the year!

And so it is in Ireland.

We have a great love and hunger for tradition. Many of these rituals came from before Christian times, were adapted by the Church, and somehow prevailed to the present day in the work and celebrations of ordinary people. When people talk today about traditions 'dying out', I generally think they are wrong. Of course, our traditions mutate and adapt to attract the attention of each new generation—but they are just too strong, soulful and rhythmic to disappear altogether.

What do you think?

As for me—I'm looking forward to our first new potatoes of the season!

That's it for now!

Slán, Mike... talk next week! :)

A Reply to Meitheamh

When I published the previous letter about the Irish midsummer, I asked readers to share a letter of their own in response. Here is one I received from Dick Godfrey—talking about his own experiences of mid-summer and that of his ancestors. Over to you, Dick:

In the twilight of the evening of June 23, 1837, William Godfrey carefully placed the four small objects in the embers of the fire he had built for the Mid-Year festival—new potatoes he had dug that morning from the rich earth of Kilcoleman, his ancestral home in County Kerry. A thin wisp of smoke from the disturbed bonfire weaved its way up towards the starry sky above, only barely diverted from its path by the soft breeze.

The beautiful night, the ancient tradition, and the fellowship of family and friends around him should have instilled the feelings of joy, love, and comfort within him, but his mind was full of trouble and doubt on this, his final Meitheamh celebration at home. Doubts of what lay ahead of him and what troubles he may find in his future in that far off land across the sea could not be stilled in his young mind.

In the twilight of the evening of June 23, 2014, James R. Godfrey, the 4th generation ancestor of William Godfrey, gently put four potatoes into the embers of his backyard fire pit in Salina, Kansas. The night sky was filled with stars and the breeze, which was unusually gentle for normally 'Windy Kansas', helped the smoke rise up to the tree tops. Around him, two of his granddaughters circled in what was their idea of a Fairy Dance, bedecked with wings and brightly coloured fairy dresses their 'Grammy' had made for them for this occasion. Looking at them with a smile, his mind travelled back to that time when his Great Grandfather must have stood before a similar fire in Ireland before he came to America. And though thousands of miles and almost 200 years separated this fire from that one, the love of the land, the traditions, and of Ireland burned deeply in his heart.

William had expressed his plans to his family and friends and tried to explain his reasons for wanting to leave the land of his birth, the little village of Milltown with all its memories, and his ancestral home of Kilcoleman. They had questioned, and pondered, and finally agreed that he should follow his dream, and so within but a few weeks he would travel down to County Cork to board a ship to the New Land.

But dreams, no matter how lofty or desirable are still dreams, and following them can have consequences. It was this thought that caused him such anguish this evening despite the excitement of the new adventure looming ahead for this 17 year old Irish youth. America was in his future...... but Eire would always be in his heart.

While eating the roasted potatoes from the fire pit James explained the tradition of the festival as much as he could to the 8 year old and 6 year olds, hoping someday he could do the same for their other six grandchildren.

Afterwards, he went out alone to cover the embers with the fire screen, and as he leaned over a small glass vial on the chain around his neck swung out into his view. He held it gently between his fingers, gazing at the grains of earth held within; grains of earth he had himself dug from the rich earth of Kilcoleman on his visit there a few years ago. To his knowledge he was the only member of the Godfrey family to have returned to Ireland since William had left there. He remembered the wonderful beauty of the land, the friendliness of the people, the excellent food and drink enjoyed in the joyful atmosphere of the places they had visited, and all the marvellous sites they had seen.

But mostly he remembered the feeling he had from the moment his feet had touched that ancient land … the overwhelming feeling that he had 'Come Home' again. A feeling that remains…

Dick Godfrey

A Methodical Approach

August 31, 2014

Céad Míle Fáilte—and welcome to your Letter from Ireland on a lovely sunny Sunday morning here in Cork. The weather has taken a turn for the better, the north winds have turned around and we might even get out for a last sea swim of the year today.

How's the weather where you are? Is it worth remarking on?

I'm having a nice cup of Lyon's tea this morning as I write—and I do hope you'll have a cup of whatever you fancy as you join me for today's 'Letter from Ireland'.

Have you ever started something—and found yourself ending up somewhere completely different to what you planned? I find this is often a feature of the Irish conversational style—a creative meandering that often delights both audience and speaker as a tale takes an unexpected turn or two. Have you noticed this?

Just this morning, I sat down to write about 'The 13 Pubs of Ballydehob'. As I pulled out my notes and started to write, I noticed something that took me on a completely different route to the one planned. So, the wonderful tales of Ballydehob and its 13 pubs will have to wait for another day.

Instead, we're going to chat (maybe for the first time) about religion in Ireland. At least one particular aspect.

Religion and Ireland—Where do you Start?

There is a saying in Ireland—'Never talk about religion or politics in the pub'—it will only end in a fight. Religion in Ireland has come to signify a lot more than a person's spiritual beliefs or church-going habits. Over the centuries, religion was the place where you made your stand—a place that stood for your culture, traditions and history. It also became a badge that locked you in—or out—of opportunity, advancement and wealth.

By 1911, we had four primary religions in Ireland. Roman Catholicism was the religion for 85% of the population. The three main Protestant religions were Church of Ireland, Presbyterianism and Methodism.

I don't know about you, but talking about religion never works for me unless we bring it down to a human level—the level of the story and the individual. So, let's do just that.

As part of my research into the '13 pubs of Ballydehob' (bear with me here!)—I examined the 1911 census for the Ballydehob area in County Cork (my own father's family was born and reared in those parts).

I was drawn in by the religions noted against each of the names on the register. The majority were Roman Catholic as you might expect, and next were Church of Ireland. Most Presbyterians are up in Ulster—so none in these parts—and next were the Methodists. And it's this last group we'll concentrate on for the remainder of this letter.

The Methodists in Ireland.

Maybe you are already familiar with 'Methodism'? The Methodists came out of the Church of England in the early 18th century, led by one John Wesley. The focus of Methodism is to help the poor and average person—building relationships and social service is at the heart of all they do.

Their methodical observance of the rules of the Book of Common Prayer regarding works of charity earned them the derogatory nickname of 'Methodists'—which they decided to keep! I do like that! The Methodists arrived in Ireland in 1747 and received most of their support, and converts, from the junior members of the British army garrisons spread throughout the country.

So, most of the Methodist converts came from Protestant stock, and a smaller number from Roman Catholic. If you converted in those days—you crossed a great divide—and mixed marriages were not condoned by society or the established churches.

Looking at the Methodist surnames in Ballydehob in 1911—you can see this mix coming through in the mostly English surnames and the smaller number of Irish Gaelic surnames:

Coy, Daly, Evans, Jennings, Johnson, Kingston, McDermott, Roycroft, Swanton, Willis, Wolfe, Woodhouse and Young.

One Special Man.

Peter Wolfe was one member of the Methodist church whom I knew. He was also Carina, my wife's, uncle. Peter married Carina's aunt in one of Ireland's first 'condoned' mixed-marriages. And that was in the 1970s.

I remember Peter as a busy man—with all the time in the world for the people around him. He ran a large business and had a young energetic family. Yet, if you needed help or assistance he gave you his full attention and enthusiastic support. He was a living embodiment of the stated intent of Methodism.

Peter died at the young age of 71 in January of this year. In all the time I have known Peter, I don't think I ever heard him talking about religion. He just did it—he somehow married the best part of his beliefs to much of what we consider important in Irish tradition. Be there for your friends, your family and your community. Be accountable and let your actions speak for themselves.

Earlier this month, his son, Mark—completed an Ironman Triathlon in Peter's memory and to raise funds for the Irish Cancer Society. He also managed to finish fourth (!!!) over a gruelling 11 hours of swimming, running a marathon and cycling around all of the Ring of Kerry. Well done Mark—a great achievement in memory of a special man. And I'm sure he was at your side all the way.

I realise that when I look up those textbook explanations of the different religions—I really don't get it. The descriptions rarely make sense to me. However, when I look at the attitude and actions of people like Peter Wolfe, I get it—the 'explanation' is there for all to see. It's all about using whatever religion you choose to let the best of your humanity shine through to others.

So, that's it for today—and to finish with that famous Irish blessing for Peter and his family—and you and all the special people in your life:

'May the road rise to meet you,

May the wind be always at your back,

May the sun shine warm upon your face,

The rains fall soft upon your fields and,

Until we meet again,

May God hold you in the palm of His hand.'

That's it for this week.

Slán for now, Mike :)

Carina's Letter

August 10, 2014

Céad Míle Fáilte—Carina here standing in for Mike on a nice warm sunny morning here in Cork. I'm afraid you'll have to put up with me today as I came downstairs earlier, pulled Mike off the keyboard and sent him back to bed. He has been sick over the past couple of weeks with recurrent food poisoning but he was still down here stressing about 'never missing a Letter from Ireland yet'. So I said, don't worry, I'll do it instead.

I'd better start with a cup of tea first and hope that you have one at hand yourself.

At this stage I read many of the replies to the Letter from Ireland each week and feel that I know everyone. I really enjoy some of the amazing stories coming back from our readers all over the world.

When I think about my own family, where they come from, lived and travelled down through the centuries, I realise that it is a very different story from so many people reading this letter. You see, apart from one amazing tale of a great grand-uncle who walked back from the Boer War in South Africa, all of my own family stayed in the same place.

My own father, a Cronin, happily travelled the world for his holidays but was always delighted to arrive home and catch up with all that was going on in the village. He left for England briefly in

88

the 1950s, but returned after 6 months and never left again. He was the only person in his family to 'emigrate'. On my mother's side, the O'Donoghues of north Cork, not one of her immediate family emigrated over the years.

I now understand that this was the way most Irish people would have liked things to be. Back to my own father—he was born in a bed over the shop he inherited and worked in most of his life. He went to school in the building next door to his house. The church and GAA pitch were just below that school. He died in the room he was born in. Yet he was very much a man of the world.

I guess that is the reality for many of your cousins, people like my father, who managed to stay in Ireland through luck or fortune.

I'll finish up by leaving in the following invitation that Mike always gives—do feel free to contact me with a question about your Irish surname, to tell a story or just to say hello!

That's it for now—short and sweet for this week!

Slán, Carina... and hopefully back to Mike next week :)

Did One of Your Ancestors Save Civilisation?

September 21, 2014

Céad Míle Fáilte—and welcome to your Letter from Ireland. The weather has broken here in Cork over the last couple of days—we had the first rainfall for a month and it's back to being cool in the mornings and evenings. But, what of it! The heat and sunshine were nice, unexpected, gifts for this late in the summer.

I do hope you are keeping well wherever you are today. I'm having a glass of water from the well this morning—keeping the body pure! So, I hope you'll have a cup of whatever you fancy yourself and join me for today's 'Letter from Ireland'.

It's going to be a bit of a free ramble in today's Letter—but with a coherent thread all the way through for those who like a signpost or two!

Are These The Most Civilised Irish Surnames?

Last week I was invited to a dinner at Dublin's Trinity College on a beautiful summer's evening. Have you been there? As dusk fell we went for a walk among the grounds before the formality of the speeches and dinner.

A sign caught my eye: 'This way for the Book of Kells'. There we were, just yards away from one of the most important illuminated manuscripts in the world—but it was safely locked up for the night. Have you seen this book? It is a marvel of art and scholarship.

The dinner itself was for a professional society—and I was sitting among a group of accountants who all knew one another. Now, I am not an accountant—but not to worry, the conversation was lively and interesting—covering most of the subjects of the day. The man sitting opposite me introduced himself as John Monaghan. The man beside me commented:

'I suppose your family came from County Monaghan originally?'

'No, actually' was the reply—*'we're County Mayo through and through'.*

'Where did the name Monaghan come from so?'

Now, that got the conversation going for me!

The Irish surname 'O'Monaghan' comes from the Irish 'Ó Manacháin' (pronounced 'Oh Man-ack-awn'). This basically means 'descendent of Manachán' or 'descendent of the little monk'.

This Irish name—Ó Manacháin—was found in various parts of the country. However:

- In Mayo and Galway—Ó Manacháin was anglicised as Monaghan.

- In Clare and Tipperary—Ó Manacháin was sometimes anglicised as Minogue.

- In Cork and Limerick—Ó Manacháin was anglicised as Mannix—sometimes Manahan.

And all these came from the same Irish surname. We wonder why Irish genealogy and surnames can be confusing!

If you held this surname, it did not necessarily mean you were the 'son of a preacher man'. You see, Manachán was a first name in use in early Christian times (it is still used today in parts of Ireland). As is the way with most first names, it was primarily descriptive. The monk was a feature on the Irish social landscape since the time before Saint Patrick. Perhaps the early holders of this name were given it because they had the countenance of a monk. Perhaps they had a similar hairline. Perhaps they embraced austerity. Perhaps they partied all day—and it was given to them in an ironic fashion!

Over time, certain holy men who held this first name became saints (e.g. Saint Munchin of Limerick) and even more babies were named Manachán in honour of this saint. And so such names proliferated until about 800 AD when Irish surnames were initiated in Ireland.

From the 800s onwards, different Irish family groups 'froze' their collective titled name in honour of an illustrious ancestor—into the surnames that we are familiar with today. One sept in the north of Connaught decided on the collective title 'descendants of Manachán' or Ua Manacháin or Ó Manacháin—which was anglised as O'Monaghan many centuries later.

Did One of Your Irish Ancestors Save Civilisation?

A clue as to why Thomas Cahill's book 'How the Irish Saved Civilization' has been such a best-seller surely has to be in the title? Could anyone with Irish ancestry resist a title like that? Maybe you have read it?

In the book, he explores how the Irish monks of the early Christian church established centres of learning across Ireland and the rest of Europe. Future kings attended these 'universities' which were located in places such as Glendalough and Clonmacnoise. Here, the local monks worked to transcribe and preserve the written works of early Greek, Roman and Irish civilisation. Their efforts and accomplishments provided Ireland with the reputation as an 'isle of saints and scholars'.

The tradition of these early Celtic monks was very different to that of the later closed-order tradition that arrived via the Roman hierarchical church (the Cistercians, Franciscans and so on).

The Celtic monastic focus was on prayer, learning and teaching. The monks often lived in communities that they shared with their own families, craftspeople and others. They looked different—not like the 'Friar Tuck' we think of today with a round bald spot at the top of his head. They typically shaved their hair for a few inches at the top of the forehead. Think 'mullet' with no fringe!

This was the type of monk that carried, and made popular, many of the Irish names we know today. Names like Brendan, Kevin, Declan, Brigid, Aidan, Colman and so on. Maybe some of these names are in your family?

So thanks to John Monaghan (of County Mayo!) who opened up this conversation about Irish given names, surnames, monastic traditions and illuminated manuscripts. It was a rich conversation—full of all that is best about our Irish history, traditions and culture.

That's it for this week.

Slán for now, Mike :

Do You See Yourself As Irish?

September 28, 2014

Céad Míle Fáilte—and welcome to your Letter from Ireland. It's a lovely Autumnal morning—a great colour in the trees, the birds are singing again and there's crispness in the air on either side of the day.

I do hope you are keeping well wherever you are today. I'm sticking to the water from the well this morning—it seems to suit the time of year! So, I hope you'll have a cup of whatever you fancy yourself and join me for today's 'Letter from Ireland'.

Yesterday, we had the All-Ireland Hurling final replay in Croke Park. Maybe you saw it? Counties Kilkenny and Tipperary were playing and it was some high-energy spectacle—but in the end Kilkenny dominated and won the game (come on the Cats!).

When I am travelling in Ireland and someone asks 'Where are you from?'— the answer expected is almost always the county you live in or grew up in. Nowadays, we have a strong affinity to our county. It's only when I travel abroad, I start to think of myself as Irish—do you know what I mean?

How Do You See Yourself?

Over on our Facebook page (www.facebook.com/youririshheritage), I asked the question: 'How do you see yourself? Irish-American? Australian? British? Anglo-Irish? Canadian?'

The reason I asked was related to an article on IrishCentral.com with the headline 'Why do people in Ireland not consider an Irish American to be Irish?' It was written by a second-generation Irish man who returned often as a boy to Ireland to be with his cousins. He saw himself as Irish—his cousins thought he was a 'Yank'.

And I must admit, I do hear different versions of this question a lot! In fact, we received a lot of comments on that Facebook post including the following from our good friend Pamela Murungi:

'... reading this almost makes me feel that if that is truly how Ireland born Irish view us Irish Americans, perhaps I don't want to see Ireland quite so badly. Seeing Ireland has been a lifelong dream, not an easy thing to consider abandoning. But you see, I've just enough German stubbornness to get defensive about not being considered Irish, and I'd want to enjoy my time in my ancestral country and not listen to how I'm not Irish.... which would be sure to get my Irish up.'

Now, you try and tell me that that lady is not Irish! First, Pamela, when the time comes to visit Ireland—you let me know if anyone doubts your Irishness and I will deal with them personally. However, I think you'll be in there before me!

An Island Of Tribes and Townlands.

In Ireland, we never really had a 'United' Kingdom. It was a land of different tribes (called Tuatha) and tribal lands for many centuries. That sense of being 'Irish' (and proud of it) only really came to the fore with the Gaelic revival in the late 1800s. At that time, we also saw the game of hurling come into being.

It was the local place from which you came that formed your identity—your extended family and the local landmarks said as much as you needed to know about who you were. With the rise of British dominance came awareness that being Irish (and Irish Catholic) was quite a negative thing. It meant poor land, subsistence living and a lack of opportunity.

After the terrible time of the famine—and the subsequent decades of emigration—the Irish abroad often found that this negative view of the Irish travelled with them. It was hard to shake. Many of our ancestors embraced the fresh start that a new nation offered—if not to them, then at least for their children.

But they always carried those Irish qualities with them—and sometimes shared them freely. Down the years accents changed, cultures intermarried and life got better—sometimes good enough to return to live in Ireland (like my own parents), or sometimes to visit cousins and relatives who met them somewhere within the full range of 'open arms' to 'indifference'.

I guess I would summarise by saying that 'Irishness' was never about borders. This has become so true over the last 150 years as the worldwide Irish ancestry population swelled to 60 million and beyond. Irishness has always been about immediate and extended family, an attitude of never giving up, a sense of decency to those around you and a love of music, stories and sharing the simple things in life.

So, if like Pamela, you are concerned that your 'Irishness' may be questioned when you meet an Irish-born native—remember to look them in the eye and show them your Irish attitude. It will happen a lot less than you imagine—but remember that it's their 'labelling' problem, not yours. Just remember that you are—and always will be—one of our own.

That's it for this week.

Slán for now, Mike :)

The Beauty of The Irish Hand

October 26, 2014

Céad Míle Fáilte—and welcome to your Letter from Ireland. The clock just 'went back' in this part of the world last night—it feels like we are officially heading into the darker time of the year.

Next week we'll be upon Halloween (or Samhain as it is called in Irish)—a real time for passing over the threshold from light to dark in Celtic cultures.

I grabbed my cup of tea to head down to the 'writing hut' this morning—and saw the most spectacular double-rainbow landing on the roof of that hut! So, there will be two pots of gold buried somewhere in today's Letter. I hope you'll join me now with your own cup of tea or coffee for a chat about one of the most beautiful legacies of Irish heritage and culture.

A Land of Saints, Scholars and Craftsmanship.

A few weeks back, I mentioned Thomas Cahill's book 'How the Irish Saved Civilisation'—and I know a lot of our readers have already come across it. It tells the story of how Irish monks set about preserving Greek, Roman and early Christian knowledge through their manuscripts and teaching. It's a wonderful little book and I heartily recommend it.

Well, some days ago, Cork University Press sent on a copy of one of their own new publications: *'The Irish Hand: Scribes and their manuscripts from their earliest times'*. I was both intrigued and delighted by what I saw.

You see, whereas reading 'How the Irish Saved Civilisation' was like gazing at a new car or coat, this new book was like going for a drive or trying it on!

The Irish Hand' was written by Ireland's leading scribe—one Timothy O'Neill—and illustrates and discusses many of the famous ancient books of Ireland. He outlines their content, scribes and patrons—shows a page from each—and talks about the old Irish writing and illustration techniques. A true gem!

The Books, Families and Lords of Ireland.

'From a shrub covert, shadow mantled

A Cuckoo's clear sing-song delight me.

O at the last, the Lord protect me!

How well I write beneath the wood'

Translated by Seamus Heaney and Timothy O'Neill

This little verse was typical of the notes written in the margins of Ireland's ancient books. They were written by the scribes as they set about their learned, artistic and back-breaking work of scribing and copying from lesser volumes—often using inferior tools and materials, and often to wondrous results.

Many of the ancient books are preserved today in libraries and museums. Some of these more famous scripts are featured in the 'The Irish Hand'. When we examine the full family of scripts, we notice that they are of very specific types. I have divided them up as follows—with a little background and a list of some of the family names associated with each:

1. Religious texts.

These were the first transcribed volumes—often the gospels, psalms or lives of saints. They were typically commissioned and written inside the old Irish monasteries by the incumbent abbots and monks.

An example is the great 'Book of Kells'.

2. The Annals, Genealogies and Sagas.

Over time, the religious texts were chronologically ordered—showing the saints' feast days and so on. Important local events for the local lordships were also noted. These evolved into 'Annals'—capturing significant births, battles, deaths and genealogies for the lords of specific areas.

An example is the 'Annals of the Four Masters'.

This type of book was often written and maintained by historian and genealogist families attached to specific lordships. Including families like O'Daly, O'Clery, O'Dugan, O'Cassidy, O'Duigenan, Keating, O'Higgins, Ward, Dunleavey, Shields, O'Flynn and even more.

Are any of your Irish family names here?

3. Legal Texts.

Ireland was governed by 'Brehon Law' up to the mid 1600s. It was a form of justice that was suited to bringing justice to family groupings. The 'Brehons' (or judges) were responsible for capturing the law, teaching apprentices and interpreting these laws for the local Tuatha and lordships.

Examples of these legal texts include the 'Senchas Már'. The chief Brehon families were Egan (MacEgan), Forbes, Neeve, O'Phelan, MacCarroll, Conway, Keenan, Coffey and Breheny/Judge.

Are any of your Irish family names here?

4. Medical Texts.

By the early 1700s, Ireland had the largest written collection of medical texts in the world. One example is 'The Book of the O'Lees'.

Like the Brehons and Poets/Historians—the medical families were typically tied to and sponsored by a particular lordship. Some of the chief medical families include: O'Cassidy, O'Lee, O'Canavan, O'Tully, O'Kearney, Dunleavey, O'Hickey and many more.

Are any of your Irish surnames here?

By the 15th century, the chief lordships of Ireland displayed their power through the sponsorship of monasteries, the commissioning of the above genealogies, poems and sagas as well as the nurturing of Brehons, Bards, Historians and medical families in their territories. It was a time of 'Gaelic resurgence'—well after the

Norman families had arrived and mostly Hibernicised—and before the arrival of the first 'planters' from England and Scotland.

These patron lordships included O'Donnell, O'Neill, O'Connor, McCarthy, Butler, Fitzgerald, Maguire, McMurrough, O'Rourke, O'Flaherty and many more.

With the protestant ascendency and English domination from the mid-17th century on, many of the Gaelic traditions, laws, genealogies and medical texts ceased to be of everyday use and significance—and instead became private collector items, spread far and wide across the world.

Thankfully, many of these priceless volumes have found their way back to public spaces like Trinity College in Dublin where they are available to both the public and scholars.

Scholars and craftsmen like Timothy O'Neill—who has captured much of the energy, beauty and wonder of this time and these manuscripts in his wonderful volume 'The Irish Hand'!

That's it for this week—the best of Irish luck to you!

Slán for now, Mike.

Is There Room for the Irish Language in Your Life?

Nov 16, 2014

Céad Míle Fáilte—and welcome to this week's Letter from Ireland. The weather here is getting wetter by the day, almost to biblical proportions at this point—a dry day seems rarer than a hens tooth.

I hear that many of our friends in North America are 'enjoying' the first snowfalls of the year all of this week. I do hope you are keeping safe and comfortable wherever you are.

I'm settling into a glass of water from the well—it's particularly sweet at the moment. I do hope you'll join me with a cup of whatever you fancy yourself—and we'll start into today's Letter from Ireland.

I must admit, I find English, the language of this letter, to be one of the most beautiful languages in the world. Down through the centuries, it stretched in the most unlikely directions taking in the beautiful words and culture of each land that it colonised.

One of these lands was Ireland—a place where the Irish language evolved over the centuries to reflect and describe the traditions and culture of our people.

Last Friday I was sitting in my car at nine in the morning. The car was not moving. Now, being stuck in a traffic jam is rarely a pleasure—but in this case I looked on in wonder as hundreds of schoolchildren made their way into a local school. It was a newly built 'Gaelscoil'—a place where all subject matter is taught through the language of Irish.

Irish is a language that went into catastrophic decline in the 17th century—and that language is the subject of our letter today.

Is There Room For The Irish Language In Your Life?

Irish is the language of stories, heroes, music, tradition, connection and family that has been used on this island of Ireland for thousands of years. We first became aware of Irish in its written form as the monks transcribed the old Latin manuscripts and wrote notes in 'Old Irish' on the margins of the pages. This was the 6th century, and the Old Irish language absorbed many Latin words through the activity of these monks.

By the 10th century, Irish had evolved into what we call 'Middle-Irish' today. This was a version spoken across the island of Ireland as well as traveling to Scotland and the Isle of Man with the Irish people of the time. Today, what we call 'Scots Gaelic' is a dialect of this Middle-Irish language.

By the seventeenth century, we get the 'Modern Irish' that is still in use today. By that time, Irish was spoken by the majority of the people of Ireland. It was not until the time of the Great Famine (An Gorta Mór – 'The Great Hunger' in Irish) that the language went into a catastrophic decline that continued until today.

However, when I look at the 1901 census records showing my great-grandfather's household, he is noted as speaking both English and Irish. This mix of languages remained common for many of our ancestors across the rural townlands of Ireland.

The Wisdom of Irish Proverbs.

The Irish language is a keen observer of nature and cycles of life and death. Much of the wisdom that was passed from generation to generation was encoded in the many Irish proverbs and blessings we know today. These proverbs are known in Irish as 'Seanfhocail' or 'old words'.

Let's explore some of the Irish language through the medium of these proverbs—maybe you have heard of some of these already? I'm sure you might even have a few more to add.

'Is buaine port ná glór na n-éan,
Is buaine focal ná toice an tsaoil.'

'A tune outlasts the song of the birds,
A word outlasts the wealth of the world.'

I like this proverb as it reminds me of the important things in life—it also underlines the value and power that the Irish place in music and the spoken word. In a way, it shows the priorities of an entire people through one proverb.

'Is maith an scéalaí an aimsir.'

'Time is a great storyteller.'

I think this is one to bear in mind as you dig deeper into your family ancestry! Over time, many stories and myths have come to surround (and enliven) what were once given facts of the day. I also like that the word 'aimsir' (pronounced 'aye-m-shir') can also mean 'weather'. As we all know, the weather can be a great trickster in Ireland!

'Mac an tsaoir ábhar an tuata.'

'The son of a craftsman may grow up ignorant of his father's skills.'

This is a timeless piece of wisdom that tells us we often don't appreciate that which is closest. But have another look. As you know, I like to chat about Irish surnames and here you see an interesting view on a particular surname. Firstly, you see 'mac'—which of course means 'son', and is the prefix for many Irish and Scottish surnames.

Next, the word 'tsaoir' (pronounced 'teer') comes from the Irish word for 'free' which equates a craftsman with a freeman. That is what a craftsman was in old Irish society—free. Finally, this 'son of the craftsman' gives us the later surnames 'MacAteer', 'Freeman' and 'MacIntyre'—all anglicisations of 'Mac an tSaoir'.

Like these surnames, much of the Irish language has survived in the shape of the Irish surnames in your family. Names such as Heffernan, Murphy, Kelly, Dineen, McNamara, O'Brien, Mannion, Cleary, Byrne, Connolly, Foley, Lynch and Doherty—just a small sample of surnames that started out in the Irish language at one stage.

Do you know your family surnames in Irish?

'An áit a bhuil do chroí is ann a thabharfas do chosa thú.'

'Your feet will bring you to where your heart is.'

Oh, I do like this one! You can dream all you want—but you do need to take the first steps and start doing! At least, that's the way I choose to read this one. How about you?

'Is gaire cabhair Dé ná an doras.'

'God's help is closer than the door.'

Many Irish proverbs give reference to God, Mary and the Saints. This seems to sit well with most Irish people who have an instinctive belief in a power and grace beyond the individual.

'Ar scáth a chéile a mhairimíd'.

'We live in the shelter of one another'

Finally, one of my favourites, which you may have heard me use more than once already. Because, it is true my friend—for people of Irish ancestry throughout the word—we share so much in our attitude and values. We truly do 'live in the shelter of one another'.

So, as I think back on those young schoolchildren lining up to enter the 'Gaelscoil' last Friday—it delights me that this great language of ours has a chance to become an essential part of our everyday lives once again.

Would you like to learn some Irish? Maybe you know a few words already.

That's it for this week—as always, do feel free to REPLY and say hello, share an Irish surname in your family—or a proverb that was often in use. Thank you again for being a part of the Letter from Ireland.

Slán for now—Mike and Carina :)

Have You Ever Had a Drop of the Irish?

Dec 7, 2014

Céad Míle Fáilte—and welcome to this weeks 'Letter from Ireland'. It's a lovely crisp, sunny morning here in County Cork as I write. I do hope the weather is treating you kindly wherever you are in the world.

I've just poured a cup of Barry's tea for myself – I'd be delighted if you'll join me now with a cup of whatever you're having, as we start into today's Letter from Ireland.

I'll Have A Drop With That!

Do you like the taste of Irish Whiskey? Maybe you like it in a 'Hot Toddy'? Or as a nice smooth base layer in your Irish Coffee?

As a young(er) fellow, I served my time as a barman in Michael Barrys' pub in Douglas, County Cork. Each evening, a few different 'auld fellows' would come in and take their regular stools at the bar. The order of the day was normally a pint of stout (or a half pint if their bladders weren't up to it!), but all of them had a 'drop on the side'.

This 'drop', or 'half one', was a half-measure of Irish whiskey. Some would take it with a jug of water, some with ginger-ale on the side—and some more would simply tip the whiskey into the creamy head of their newly poured pint. The height of drinking efficiency.

During this time, the 1970s, the choice of Irish Whiskeys was at it's lowest for centuries. You had a choice of brands called 'Powers' or 'Paddy'—or maybe 'Bushmills', 'Jameson' or 'Hewitt' if you were feeling a little more exotic. But, Irish whiskey was clearly dying out with these auld fellows—and the feeling was that it might soon be gone.

A Brief History of The Water of Life.

The English word Whiskey comes from the Irish 'Uisce Beatha' (pronounced 'ish-ka ba-haa')—literally meaning 'Water of Life'. It is believed that the process for distilling whiskey was introduced into Ireland around 1000 AD by Irish monks who were already familiar with the distilling process used for perfumes on the continent of Europe. Shortly after, these monks also introduced the distillation of whiskey to their monasteries in Scotland. Those monasteries were cold places!

Over time, the smoother whiskeys of Ireland were considered much superior to Scottish whisky and for a number of centuries, Irish whiskey was the most popular spirit in the world. By 1900, about twelve million cases were shipped from Ireland around the world.

But, then we had prohibition in the USA, the Irish war of

Independence and a series of economic and supply shocks that reduced the production of Irish whiskey all the way down to 500,000 cases by the time my 'auld fellows' were knocking back their drop from the bar stools of Mick Barrys.

In the meantime, the whiskies of Scotland—'Scotch'—had gone in the opposite direction. The number of Scottish distilleries increased—along with the quality and demand.

And then something happened.

Irish Whiskies Come Back To Life.

Since about 1993, Irish whiskey has become the fasted growing spirit drink in the world with the backing of the big conglomerates. Both the smooth-blended whiskies (such as Jameson), as well as local whiskies that have a unique character of their own, have driven this charge back onto the shelves of our pubs and off-licences. It looks like we'll be back to our previous high of 12 million cases by 2020.

But, I also think there is an interesting parallel story behind this resurgence of Irish Whiskey—and it is a personal opinion.

You know how we often chat about the catastrophic decline in the population of most Irish counties between the census of 1841 and the census of 1961? In a lot of these counties, the population was reduced by two-thirds due to famine and emigration. This was a time when many of your own ancestors left these shores for a better life.

By the late 1800's, Ireland was just starting to regain a sense of Gaelic identity—an identity that had been beaten down and forbidden for many centuries. Today, Ireland is a young country—not yet one hundred years as an independent nation. It has taken many decades to develop both a confidence in our abilities and a pride in our heritage—without feeling that we have to ask someone elses permission first.

I feel that it is only since the 1990s that we have regained a proper sense of national identity and confidence about where we stand on the world stage. As we looked back, we realised what a rich culture and set of traditions we possessed. This slowly building realisation and confidence has started to produce many examples of a resurgent Irish spirit, including the rebirth of the Irish Whiskey industry. What do you think?

So, no matter what your opinions on alcohol, whiskies—or the correct measure for an Irish Coffee—I wish you 'Sláinte' and many years of health and happiness!

Slán for now—Mike and Carina :)

Section 5: Our Readers Letters from Ireland

Introduction to this Section.

You may have noticed that the title of this book is 'A Letter from Ireland'. Most of the letters are written by myself each Sunday morning and sent out to our readers around the world.

However, many of those readers write back! They share stories, family history and ask questions of all shapes and manner.

Earlier this year, we decided to have a competition. We asked our readers to write their own Letter from Ireland.

Use your imagination we suggested.

- It might be a letter from you in Ireland back home to your family—telling them about your experiences and the sights you see.

- It might be real or imagined.

- It might be set in the past or the present.

- Up to you—use your imagination!

Here is a short selection of the letters that came back. I hope you enjoy our 'Readers Letters from Ireland'!

A Letter to my Ancestor

This letter was sent in by Jack Coffey from Canada.

In the letter, he imagines how a letter home from his ancestor may have been written—he then pens his own response across the years.

Hello, my name is Lawrence Kavanagh and I am a friend of Padrick Coffey who has asked me to write this letter for him as he cannot read nor write. His Irish Gaelic is very strong and I might miss a few words but here is what he asked me to write for him….

August 25, 1816, To my descendants whomever they be,

I have decided to leave my home in County Cork and have sailed to Canada this past season. Things are not good back home, and I do not believe they will improve. The Napoleonic wars have ceased and there is less demand for the goods that we produce. I know that I would never be able to own any land, as most of it is under control of rich Englishmen who tax us to death on what we occupy. We can never seem to get ahead.

My dear wife, Judith and I got married last September in her church in Kilbrittain. Father John Foley married us. Judith and I met a while back one Saturday when she was helping her father with his cows at the Shambles market up on Kilbrogan Hill in Bandon. She is a very pretty girl and very kind. I spent a lot of time courting her down along the river, and we often meet on the bridge in the evenings.

The rain this year was terrible, crops not doing well, and the muck is up to our knees. When we told our parents that we were thinking about crossing the ocean to a new land where the government is giving land away for free, her mother cried, but her father understood that I would not be able to get much cobbler work, and would never have a farm, so he told us to go. Both our parents are sad, they know they will probably never see us again. I promised them I would take good care of her.

Now that we have arrived in our new country we will look for a land grant and start our family. Judith and I want to farm and I can find work in my trade, I can use my musket to hunt deer and rabbit for food, I will fish in the nearby lakes for trout, cod, salmon, smelt, oysters and mussels. The winters are long and cold here, but the summers can be hot enough to have good crops, and the vast forests have enough timber to last forever. I feel in my heart I have made a good decision.

X. Padrick Coffey

April 15, 2010. Bandon, Ireland.

Dear Great great grandfather;

Where are you? I am your great, great, grandson from Canada. I have just arrived in County Cork on Air Lingus. I know you spent a month on a ship to get to Canada and I was here in five hours. I am looking for your and my roots. My, my! Your family is hard to find. I have searched the internet for hours trying to find something you may have left behind to show that you were here. I have visited the church in Kilbrittain where you and Great Great Grandmother were married. I have talked to many people in my efforts to find your trail. I know you have left something or someone behind and I will keep searching.

Love, your great, great grandson, John.

(Jack Coffey).

A Letter to my Children

This letter was sent in by Brandy Wilson from the U.S. It's a lovely colourful letter with beautiful descriptions of her experiences as well as the sights she encountered on her journey.

My Dear Children,

I am having a great time in Ireland and wish you were here to see its beauty with me. As soon as I got off the plane I had a calming feeling of being home. I am staying here in Limerick City but traveling as much of the country in my rental car as I can. It takes a bit of getting used to driving on the other side of the road.

The colours here are so vibrant and beautiful. I love how they are not afraid to have vibrant colours on their houses. Everything in America looks so uniform and drab after coming here. The grass looks greener, the sky bluer, and the flowers are so much more colourful.

The history to be seen and learned is amazing. I had a friend take me around Limerick in the car telling me about all of it. He showed me bullet holes that are still in some of the buildings from the war, and told me how the opposing sides would set up on opposite sides of Limerick River and shot back and forth at all hours. I have taken so many pictures to show you when I get home.

After my walk around Limerick I drove to many different spots.

First was Blarney Castle, I didn't make it up to the Blarney stone because I was so taken with the grounds (Rock Close) that I spent most of my time walking them. There is a beautiful little water fall, a witches kitchen, wishing steps (which I was too afraid to attempt the challenge), Druids' cave, witch stone (which comes alive at night!), fairy glade, and so much more. I did make it into the castle itself, but I just didn't go all the way to the stone at the top. Maybe next time I will get up there.

We will have to bring a lot of supplies for Samantha to do her gravestone rubbings. There are so many awesome old cemeteries here. There is one headstone in particular I would love for you to do a rubbing of. It is at the Hill of Tara. I took a picture but the weather has made it pretty much unreadable, I believe it is from the 1700s.

Other places I have visited are Lough Gur, St Flannan's Church, Ardee, Long woman's grave, Carlingford Castle, and lots more on my drives. Two weeks just isn't enough time for me to see it all like I'd like. When I come back (with you guys I hope) the stay will have to be longer. I'm thinking that we can do some self-guided touring but also have some touring with a hired guide to make sure we don't miss anything. Also, we will try to do some research to see if we can find where William Moore came from so that we can see that part of our history while here.

I love driving around and seeing the signs in Gaelic. Most are in English and Gaelic but when you get to the smaller towns they are usually only in Gaelic. That is a language I am going to have to learn. I have also been in one 'Irish traffic jam'. A farmer was moving his cows from one pasture to the other across the street. I will admit it was one time I didn't mind being stuck in traffic. The weather here is mild so it is enjoyable. It is similar to our Michigan lake affect weather but I think the wind gets a little stronger here being as it is surrounded by water on all sides. I will sign off for now to get this posted and can't wait to show you all the pictures I took when I get home.

Love,

Mom.

(Brandy Wilson).

A Short Letter Home

This is a short and sweet letter from Pat Mikels—capturing her strongest memories as she gets ready to board a plane to return home to the U.S.

As I sit here in my hotel room in Limerick waiting for my ride to get to the Shannon airport, I can't help thinking about the ten days I've been here. I saw so much of this beautiful island that my ancestors called home. I think I went through at least half of the counties in the Republic of Ireland and with our guide from Tipperary, discovered so much of the history but definitely leaving me with a thirst for more. I don't think I've seen more beautiful scenery anywhere! And the ice cream at Supermac's was divine!

We went off the beaten path many times and adjusted our itinerary if we found ourselves close to something our guide thought we would like to see. We loved seeing the sheep come up right on the road, the peat that had been cut and stacked, the bog cotton, and the flowers! I could go on and on! I will be taking many memories home with me but the highlight has to be the people. They are so warm and welcoming and friendly! And the smiles! They were everywhere! I'm already looking forward to my next trip to Ireland. And some day I look forward to finding out exactly which part of this beautiful place my ancestors called home. So, as I sit here with a smile on my face as I reflect, I know I have a connection here which will never be broken.

Sláinte! (Patricia Mikels).

A Letter to my Grandmother

Patti Daly decided to write a letter to the Grandmother she never met—but seemed to know all the same!

Dear Grandma Margaret, (or I guess Maggie as they used to call you!)

I know I never got the chance to meet you, since you passed just before I was born, but I felt your love through my father, and I hope you have felt my love right back.

After many years of researching my family and yours, I had the chance of a lifetime to visit the Emerald Isle called Ireland! I couldn't believe anyone would want to leave such a beautiful place, but I know times were tough and your mother wanted nothing but the best for you, so she sent you on your way for a better life, and actually, I am glad she did.

From our first steps off the jet after a long trip, I could tell the Irish were some of the friendliest people I had met. After gathering our things we made our way down to Tramore where you called home. I stood on Cove Road where you grew up, walked up and down the street that I know you had travelled, saw where you had once lived and tried to imagine what it looked like through your eyes. Then we went to Doneraile Walk where your brother Richard's family had their home and looked out over the sea, thinking all the time this is what you saw.

Of course a trip wouldn't be the same if we didn't go to Dunhill Castle, the Power Clan castle. Ok, it isn't really a castle now, but we had to see where our ancestors hundreds of years ago had once lived.

We went to the church where you worshiped and found the cemetery where your father and family are laid to rest. The four of us split up and said, 'when you see a Power or Fitzgerald yell out!' Well, we all started yelling. I know, practically the whole cemetery was the name Power or Fitzgerald. We have such original names! Even though we were told there wasn't a headstone for your father, we said some prayers for all of them.

Of course we had to hit a pub, and even though I don't drink I had to try something. Yes, the Irish are the friendliest people on earth!

When it was time to leave, we said good-bye to your brother Edward's granddaughter who was kind enough to show us around the Waterford area and promised to make our way back. Thousands of miles apart and we can still feel like we are home and with family.

Thank you grandma Maggie, for making us proud to have Irish blood in our veins and to be able to call Ireland home!! Until we meet again!

Your loving granddaughter,

Patti.

(Patti Daly)

A Letter Home to my Family

Mary Leidner from the US received the wonderful gift of a trip to Ireland from her children. In this letter, she brings them up to date with the sights, sounds and experiences of that trip of a lifetime.

My Dear Family,

We boarded our Aer Lingus flight to Shannon at Baltimore Washington International Airport (a 65th birthday Present from our six children). Ron and I are full of expectations of what we imagine Ireland to be. This is our dream come true. As we circle to land at Shannon Airport, a look below reveals the loveliest green landscape.

As we deplane in Shannon the first person we encounter smiles and says 'Welcome to Ireland can I help you find your ride'? What a wonderful surprise. As we move toward our transportation no one seems to be in a hurry. Our C.I.E. tour driver welcomes us to begin our 10 day tour of Ireland. We will be staying several more days on our own at the end of this first visit. We are spending our first day in Dublin strolling around the city. I can't believe how friendly the people are. Everywhere we go everyone is so welcoming and helpful. They stop whatever they are doing to help us find our way. We left our hotel in search of the Temple Bar (we thought it was a Pub not a whole district.)

As we walked along a young man strolling beside overheard our discussion as to where we were going and offered to walk us to the Temple Bar which was in the opposite direction he had been going. We invited the young man to join us for a pint but he said 'the wife was expecting him 2 hrs. earlier, but we should just say hello in the bar and many would be happy to join us. In Dublin we learned how to pour the perfect pint of Guinness. Beer tastes the best in Ireland. We had lunch at the O'Neill pub. I really enjoyed seeing my family name on the storefront. I think the O'Neill name in Ireland is as common as Smith or Jones in the USA.

There is so much history on this small Island that one could spend a lifetime investigating it and write several books about the experience. I had wanted to track my O'Neill family but every town and village we visited it seems had an O'Neill prominent in their history. For example when we visited Kinsale the O'Neills and O'Donnells of Ulster in 1601 defeated the Irish Culloden which led to the Flight of the Earls. Most of these towns and villages have survived from medieval times.

This trip we are visiting many of the tourist venues in Ireland, including Dublin Castle, Jameson Whiskey, where Dad became a certified Irish whiskey taster. Trinity College and the wonderful Book of Kells, The Abbey Tavern in Howth, enjoying grand Irish music and dance, The Rock of Cashel and many more too numerous to mention. Ireland is so rich in history which has influenced the world.

When we travelled to Blarney Castle, we encountered a wedding party on their way to their wedding in Killarney. They permitted us to take their picture and then invited us to the wedding. So many villages each with friendly people and more beautiful than the last. There was Kenmare, Clonakilty (home of Michael Collins) where we enjoyed a seaside flea market. Everywhere there were lovely green fields dotted with sheep, goats, and beef cattle, shepherds walking the fields in their knicker-suits with dogs watching the flocks and lovely blooming azaleas and rhododendrons in full bloom. Ireland certainly is a 'little bit of heaven'. We felt as if we were time travelling back in the 21st century.

The Kerry Bog gave us our first taste and the history of Irish coffee and then on to Killarney. Our good friend in America Patrick McNulty was born and raised in Killarney and at age 91 told me 'none is so beautiful as the Lakes of Killarney' and he is right. They are breath-taking.

When you ask me 'what was so great about Ireland'? My response is EVERYTHING. The people treat us as if we are family always welcoming and helpful. Irish history is beautiful, awful, inspiring and poetic. It is extremely difficult to describe Ireland in just a few paragraphs. We suggest to our children and grandchildren that you take a trip to Ireland, Any location will do because each has its own beauty and charm and wonderful people. I learned in Ireland about a great inheritance which I received from my ancestors, the gift of gab. Dad says I never shut up and it takes me a very long time to tell a story.

I see humour in everything and I always wondered why I am that way. During this our first trip to Ireland I now know why. It's my Irish Blood.

My creative side is another gift from Ireland. I believe that the Irish were scattered to the four corners of the earth by God, to make the world a better place. They never forget their roots and accept everyone with a grand welcome. All over the world they still share their love of music and art and storytelling. They teach us by their actions that each of us is important in this world.

So many wonderful sights and memories.

In conclusion, Dad and I feel as if we will never see all of Ireland and yet we have seen it all because it is beautiful beyond description, the most welcoming country in the world. The final gift from Ireland is that it has shared its people with all the world in order to make us all a little bit Irish.

Mary.

(Mary Leidner).

My Emails Home

Jane Dougan from the US decided to go all 'hi-tech' on us! Here she has collected some short and catchy updates on email—her way of keeping in touch with the folks back home.

9/07/09 Greetings all from Ireland!

Wish you all were here!! There's so much to share, I don't know where to begin. I'll try to send a longer email another time soon. We've seen beautiful scenery, have a fun tour guide and a lot of nice people on the bus.

Tried my Guinness and I like it!

Tomorrow we go to the Slieve League cliffs, the highest cliffs in Europe. Today we went to Beleek Pottery and saw how similar their trade is to the dental lab.

More later—love to all.

9/08/09 Greetings again,

The Slieve League cliffs are breath-taking, they remind us of Big Sur in California! We met some Doyles in a town called Kells. We were in Donegal last night and a local said there are McNultys up the street. One of the McShanes that was driving a shuttle said welcome brother to Rob when he was told it was a family name

(Bob Dougan's mother was a McShane).

More later… Love to all ~

9/13/09—Greetings all,

As we are approaching our last day in Ireland…with mixed feelings I reflect. We saw the Ring of Kerry yesterday and it was much like a peninsula of 'Big Surs.' The mountains, and the water and the 40 shades of green are awe inspiring. More than anything the biggest impact might be the people. Everything reminds me of that Frank McNulty character, (My Dad), the roots that so many of us have here and all the Irish names. They are friendly, funny and as we saw a taste of the Irish temper the other day, sometimes fierce, but always passionate.

We heard Irish music like the Isle of Tears which reflects the impact of the Great Famine where they lost almost half of their population to death or emigration. But through it all the tremendous Irish 'pride' has survived as we saw during the final song in the pub in Killarney the other night, everyone rose to their feet and sang Ireland's national anthem.

We head to Blarney today then back to Dublin for our stay in a Castle. Looking forward to seeing you all soon and sharing memories and pictures!

Love, love, love to all, Jane.

(Jane Dougan).

How Ireland Has Changed

Barbara Skwarski from the US compares the Ireland of today with that which she saw on her first visit in 1968.

I don't have to tell you how beautiful Ireland is, all of us have been here.

I was just thinking about our first visit 'home' in 1968. It had been 20 years since Mom and Dad had seen their relatives, and much had changed. Remember the differences between staying at Mamo's in the West of Connemara and Uncle Thomas' Dairy Farm in Clare? Mamo didn't have electricity or running water, which we thought was great fun, pumping the 'tiley' for light and heating rain water over the fire to wash up-our hair never felt silkier! The 'can-o-pee' bed was a different story. Some people had a canopy over their bed, we had one under the bed!

'Helping' Uncle Thomas save the hay was also fun for us, and though I'm sure he could have done without the help of a pack of Yank kids, he was very patient and kind with us. I can still feel the warm of the sun and breeze coming from Loop Head not far away.

Ireland has changed, as the Beatles song says 'some forever not for better', but that is the way life is, and no country knows better or has experienced more change than dear sweet Ireland. Invaded, thrown off their land, starved, and yet both sides of our family stayed and toughed it out. We have no idea the desperation our ancestors felt, or the sadness. You have only to visit a mass grave site to feel the sadness, or Kilmainham and the GPO to feel their spirit and sacrifice against oppression.

Yet they survived, and more than that they THRIVED! Mom and Dad have told us so many stories about the house parties, the music, the laughter, the sheer joy of being Irish and free, and living off the land. Sometimes with all our modern conveniences, I envy them that joy and freedom. I asked Mom and Dad many times how they survived, and Mom would simply say 'Sure, we didn't know any better' I didn't understand that at first, but I do now. You survived, you thrived, because failure was NOT an option. Make the best of your circumstances.

I'll close by saying, I am thoroughly enjoying the fresh and wonderful food, the sad and inspiring music and the majesty of the sea, the mountains, rolling fields and the cliffs. There is nothing like sitting at the edge of the Wild Atlantic, watching the waves crash and imagine Dado taking his small boat into the surf to fish, and the millions of Irish who looked back on the shore, broken-hearted, never to smell the sea, or a turf fire again. Yet, here I am, because of the bravery of our parents to set off to a new life in a new land, here I am, fierce fat as the Irish would say, proud and sad at the same time, and I wouldn't have it any other way!

See you soon, Love, Barbara.

(Barbara Skwarski).

Kindness is not an Act, It is a Lifestyle

Colleen Barrett Lunt wrote home about her recent trip to Ireland—and the unexpected kindness and help she received along the way. I must say, I am delighted that she had such a wonderful time—she is an example of someone who will always get the best from Ireland. Get lost often, take your time—and always ask someone for help. That's often the best 'plan' for visiting, and experiencing, the real Ireland. Over to you Colleen.

I am writing this letter for all the people who have not been to Ireland, and to the people who yearn to return to Ireland! I recently read a quote that said 'kindness is not an act. It is a lifestyle'. I hope to give some examples of this quote in my letter.

My grandparents emigrated to the State of Maine in 1912. I spent several years researching my elusive Barretts/Walshes. With a trip planned to Ireland, I felt I need more help to knock down some of my 'brick walls'. So I turned to Mike Collins of Your Irish Heritage. He, in turn, directed me to Noreen of Hibernia Roots. These were my first experiences with Irish kindness. Mike responded back to me immediately as did Noreen. This gave me a little ray of hope that I might find out some information about my family before my trip.

My sister, cousin and myself left for Ireland on May 16th. Noreen of Hibernia Roots had communicated numerous times about her progress. Then 3 weeks before we left she sent me a 14 page report. In this report she detailed my Grandmother Walsh's siblings and their names with baptism dates, churches, graveyards and their locations.

So our heritage tour was underway with our new founded information! We arrived very early on a Saturday morning. As our plane made its approach to the Shannon airport, I could see the sunrise shimmering on the tile rooftops below. It looked just like gold! I knew right then that this trip was going to be magical! The kindness acts continued…from the car rental lady upgrading our rental from a Toyota Corolla to a Mercedes at no extra charge! To our cottage landlord in Kinsale, who had tea and scones waiting for us upon our arrival. The warmth and kindness continued through the week, from the merchants and employees at the pubs. It was not uncommon to have directions drawn out for us on a piece of scrap paper!!

The main purpose of our trip was to visit the towns our grandparents lived in. We had no knowledge of any living relatives. But we were thrilled to visit a few churches, towns and graveyards. On one of our trips to a graveyard, we realized we were in the wrong one. A lady who was visiting the graveyard offered to show us the correct one, and she told us after we would go to her house for tea! Well, we are from the states where it is unusual to invite strangers into your home! But she trusted us so in turn we trusted her. We had a delightful time, she served tea, brown bread and barbeque salmon. I thought to myself this is the way life should be! The warmth, trust and kindness that was extended to us was certainly very special.

We experienced some very unusual acts of kindness such as

when there were 24 cars behind us on a very winding narrow road. We pulled over at the soonest opportunity, as they passed us the drivers were very polite as if to say we understand!

The absolute highlight of our trip was when we travelled to my grandmother's birthplace. Noreen had found that Catherine Walsh was born and baptised in Ovens Ireland in 1869. Noreen had also found her 6 siblings, their bd's and baptisms. As we headed off to find the church in Ovens, of course we got lost! We stopped to ask directions and this young woman offered to take us to the church, and gave us her phone number just in case we got separated on the 2 mile trip!

When we arrived at the church, the young woman gathered the other mothers who were waiting for their children. Before we knew it there were several young ladies on their cell phones calling the Priest, the town historian, and the lady who has the church records. The town historian arrived to give us a tour of the church. To imagine that my grandmother was baptised in this church was amazing! During the tour a lady walked down the centre isle holding the baptism records from 1869. This lady's name was Mary, and she pointed, as she opened the book, to my grandmother's name. It showed her parents, and witnesses! Well needless to say, there were tears , laughter and amazement! We had been trying to locate this document for a long time…and there it was.

This only took place because of the kind young ladies calling people on their cell phones! As we talked to the town historian, we learn that he had just left his dialysis treatment to come to the church to help us! We were absolutely speechless, how all these strangers embraced us …with no questions asked! Mary filled out the forms that we needed, at no cost. She then mentioned that she knew some Walshes in town. I asked for some names and compared them to the ones that Noreen had given. There were some common names! Mary suggested that we should go and meet the people. All we had to do was 'go to the end of the road and take a left at the pub'! Well, off we went, and to our surprise we met our Walsh cousins! We spent the rest of the day, and all of the next day. They showed us the old homestead along with the grave of our great grandparents. This was a special experience, because of the kindness of the folks back at the church. How beautiful!

We feel extremely blessed with our experience. There were so many people that played a part in the outcome. The common theme is kindness, and I really feel that kindness is a life style in Ireland. I feel very passionate about the heritage tourism idea for Ireland. I feel people could certainly benefit—both from Ireland and abroad.

This beautiful country has survived many hard times over the years. And its people still remain trusting, warm, and most of all kind. Thank you Ireland for renewing my faith!

Best Regards,

Colleen.

(Colleen Barrett Lunt)

Conclusion

I hope that you enjoyed this edition of a Letter from Ireland. If you would like to receive a Letter from Ireland each week, you can sign up for free at:

www.youririshheritage.com/letterfromireland

Slán for now,

Mike Collins.

Appendix.

Irish Ancestry Research— When to Hire a Genealogist

Irish Genealogy can present a lot of 'brick walls' as you progress with the research into your Irish family history. I often get emails from people asking if they should hire a genealogist based in Ireland—and wondering how to go about it.

So, I got in touch with Noreen Maher of Hibernia Roots and asked her some questions that we frequently come across in our reader forum.

The purpose of this interview was to:

- Look at Irish family history research from the perspective of an active Genealogist on the ground.

- Provide you with a means of deciding when, if ever, is the right time to seek the professional help of a genealogist in your family research.

So—here are the questions—and answers!

Mike: What attracted you to becoming a Genealogist?

Noreen: It all started with me researching my husband's family after my mother-in-law died—my son is the youngest grandchild and I wanted him to know more about his paternal side. I had a lot of skills and experience that made it a natural choice for me. Once I got started I realised I didn't know where to find information, apart from the Irish census online.

I decided to sign up for a course to learn how to research and ended up studying for a Diploma run by the Association of Professional Genealogists of Ireland. It's addictive!

M: What are the special challenges when Tracing your ancestors in Ireland—for both the individual and Genealogist?

N: For individuals, it's the fact that every day new databases are coming online. There are so many sources that it is difficult to know which one is best or most reliable. However, there are still so many records, and documents that are still held locally such as church parish registers etc. —whose digital release are delayed due to lack of funding. It can be frustrating, hearing an announcement of a planned release date and you watch that date pass you by!

For genealogists, it's probably the fact that we lost a huge treasure of records—including the earlier census forms which were destroyed in fire during the Irish Civil War in 1922. It means we have to be more resourceful—obscure documents and records such as land records, electoral rolls, petitions and so on take on a more valuable role as 'census substitutes'.

M: What sorts of situations/brickwalls cause a person to call you and say 'I need help'?

N: TV shows make genealogy look easy but in fact you need to be a 'project manager'—meaning analytical, organised, and focused on the task. Many people start out by looking for someone famous in their family. They have heard stories and want to prove a connection but don't really know how to go about researching their family tree. It can be overwhelming with so much available on line. Because of the internet, people feel research can be done at a 'mouse click' from your sofa.

But with Irish genealogy, it is only realistically possible to trace ancestors back to the late 1700s—unless your ancestors were landed gentry. Most of the Irish that emigrated, were of the poorer classes who had no choice but to leave. Record keeping wasn't a priority and most of the tenants on land or working class had poor levels of education—most unable to read or write. On top of that, records may have been destroyed or no longer exist. All of these factors can bring your research to a halt.

However, a good genealogist will be able to assess the case, review the family's research so far, check to see if any records exist for the time period and then guide them to the next step or take over the project to completion. In the last 10 years, people have become more affluent but also pressed for time. A genealogist can cut through all the information and sources and will be up to date on the latest releases and availability of records—they then use a tried and tested methodology to produce a report.

To engage a genealogist too early is a bad idea as it can raise expectations. A genealogist needs some facts, family names, dates etc. to start with. I always suggest that a potential client starts with themselves and works back—to look at their own family records such as birth or marriage certificates, gravestone inscriptions and any family documents such as wills or photographs. If they can trace back to their ancestors arrival in their new country whether it's the U.S, Canada or Australia they are then ready to move the research to Ireland.

M: I have noticed that some people are wary of spending

money and getting nowhere with a Genealogist. What do you say to them?

N: Most Irish genealogists offer a free assessment as a starting point. If there are insufficient records existing for the family, then I inform my client whether it is feasible to progress to a report. Only at that stage is payment required.

I am always willing to tailor my research to the specific requirements of the family. However, there are occasions when a genealogist has to spend time searching for family members with negative results. Sometimes that is exactly what the client needs— to prove or disprove the existence or verify a story passed down in the family. But a minority of clients may not appreciate a negative result.

M: What should a person look for when they are looking to engage a Genealogist in Ireland?

N: When you engage a genealogist you are handing over your family records and anecdotes and entrusting them to the care of the genealogist. You should check the genealogist's credentials.

Always check their website—does their style or approach appeal to you? Once you make the initial contact, do you feel a rapport— do you feel that the genealogist understands your needs? How flexible are they or do they have set report packages? Are their pricing structures visible? The National Library of Ireland and the National Archives of Ireland hold lists of both genealogists and researchers on their website.

M: Can you give a couple of examples of the work that you were happiest (or surprised) with?

N: A client knew his grandfather was in the Royal Irish

Constabulary (Irish Police force pre-1922)) but little was known in the family or talked about. By obtaining a copy of his eldest child I (and the family) was surprised to see that he was also in the Royal Irish Fusiliers and released from the RIC to serve in France in the First World War. He survived and was readmitted to serve in the RIC until it was disbanded in 1922. I managed to find his military medal card record and his RIC service record.

Another client asked me to find out about her paternal grandmother's death. Her father was reared by his paternal grandparents and only knew she died young and as his father had to work, the child was left with his paternal grandparents. I discovered her grandmother died of TB aged 19, a few weeks after giving birth to a daughter who only survived about an hour. Nobody in the family knew there was a second child. It is a tragic story but bitter sweet, finally knowing what happened.

I submerge myself in every case I deal with—and it can be very emotional finding out what happened. I still get personally involved in each one as if they were my own family! It's great when I find a batch of records and put the final pieces of the jigsaw together.

M: Finally, can you share your top 3 time-saving tips if someone still really wants to carry out their own ancestry search by themselves.

N: My Top 3 Tips—especially for people who are getting started are:

1. Start with yourself and work back in a direct line—one family side at a time.

2. Identify free genealogy websites which hold information you are seeking.

3. Keep records and notes as you go along—either hard

copy or on the many online family tree databases (some free, others subscription-based).

Finally, when you have got this far—but still hit brickwalls—remember it is always a good idea to involve others. You would be surprised just how well a genealogist can help you to get unstuck—and set you off again on the right direction!

Thank you to Noreen Maher of www.hiberniaroots.com

The Surnames and Counties of Your Irish Heritage

One of the things we invite our readers to do when they want to find out more about their Irish Heritage, is to pass on the names of their ancestors and the counties they come from (if known). We have been doing this since 2013 and now have over 10,000 individuals on the list.

Here are the names that were submitted. Bear the following in mind as you scan through the names:

- They are segmented by county of origin (NOT necessarily where a surname originally came from, but where the reader says their ancestor came from). This means that some names will appear in multiple counties.

- You will see just what percentage of our total list of names came from each of the 32 counties.

- I have included the population of each county in 1841 (when the population was at its highest across most of the island) and 1961 (when the population was at it's lowest). This gives you an idea of the relative size of each county as well as the effect of famine and emigration on the population between those two years.

- Finally, I have also included a large number of 'don't know' counties of origin. These are from readers who just don't know where their ancestors lived before

144

emigration.

Please do have a look and see if you can find the Irish names in your family. If you want to add a name, just email me at **mike@youririshheritage.com**—include your own name as well as the names you want to add and the counties they come from.

County Antrim

4.8% of our reader's ancestors came from County Antrim. The county had a population of 361,000 in 1841. This had increased to 690,000 by 1961 (this is complicated by the later creation of the 'County borough of Belfast'—I included it here as part of County Antrim).

County Antrim has the distinction of having the highest number of different surnames on the island of Ireland. In other counties, there are many dominant Irish Gaelic surnames that cover percentages of the population. However, Antrim has a history of being 'planted' by individual families carrying many distinct surnames from Scotland and England.

Here are the names submitted by our readers for County Antrim—they believe that their ancestors lived in this county before emigration:

Adair Adams Agnew Alexander Allen Allingham Anderson Armour Arrells Baird Barnard Barnett Barry Beggs Black Blair Blaney Bourke Bovill Boyd Braidley Brown Brownley Bryston Butler

Caldwell Calhoun Carney Close Compton Connolly Coogan Corry Craig Crawford Creary Crossett Crowe Cubitt Culbertson Cunningham Curistan Curran

Darragh Devlin Dinsmore Dixon Dobbin Donnelly Dougherty Duffy Dunbar Earl Entrikin Ferguson Ferral Forsythe Fosters Frost Gahan Gaunt Gibson Gilman Gilmore Gilmour Gilpin Gorman Graham Green Gribbin Griggs Guinn

Hamilton Haney Harland Hawthorne Hazlett Henry Hewitt Higgensen Hill Hughes Hull Humes Humphrey Hurson Irvine Jackson Jamieson Jamison Johnston Kell Kelley Kelly Kenneally Kennedy Kernahan Keys Knox

Larkin Laughlin Laverty Lavery Law Leatham Leighton Leith Lemon Letson Logue Lucas Lynn MacKeon Mackle Magill Maids Malone Marshall McAleese McAteer McAuley McBride McBurney McCaffery McCambridge McCann McCaugherty McClain McClements McClure McCluskey McConaghey McConaghie McConnell McConway McCormick McCrary McCrum McCurdy McCurry McDonald McDonnell McDowell McDuff McElwee McFall McFarlane McGee McGinnis

McGowan McGrattan McHenry McIlhatton McIlvenny McIlwee McKay McKechnie McKeegan McKeeman McKeever McKelvie McKendry McKenzie McKeown McKillop McLaughlin McMullan McNair McQuillan McSpadden McVeigh McWilliams Meechan Meek Miller Moffat Molyneux Moore Morgan Morrow Mulholland Neill Noble

O'Boyle O'Connor O'Hara O'Kaine O'Kelley O'Malley O'Neill O'Niel O'Reilly Palmer Patterson Peden Perry Porter Quinn Ralston Reilly Reynolds Riddle Ritchie Rock Ryan Scally Scott Sharkie Sheridan Short Simpson Sinclair Slattery Smyth Smythe Spence Stephenson Stevenson Stewart Stirling Strain Strawbridge Stuart Taggert Telford Thompson Todd Toole Traynor Trimble Twigg Wales Walker Watson Weatherup White Whiteford Wilson Youngue

County Armagh

2.2% of our reader's ancestors came from County Armagh. The county had a population of 232,000 in 1841. This had declined to 117,000 by 1961.

A very ancient part of Ireland—home to many of our myths and contains the cathedral city of Armagh. Here are the names submitted by our readers for County Armagh—they believe that their ancestors lived in this county before emigration:

Armstrong Atkinson Barbour Barron Black Blackburn Blackie Blevins Calvert Canavan Cassidy Caulfield Clarke Collogly Connelly Cordner Creary Crozier Culley Curran Davitt Devine Devlin Donnelly Doyle Dunlop Eldon English Farmer Finnegan Flanagan

Gallagher Gamble Gibson Gilbonney Gillon Gilpin Graham Greenaway Greer Gregory Grier Haddock Hamilton Hinton Hughes Hunter Irwin Johnston Keady Keenan Kerrigan Kinman Lennon Lonsdale Mackle MacTavish Magee Magill Maguire Martin McArdle McCabe McCalla McCamley McCann McCarron McCartin McConnell McConville McCoy McCrum McDonald McGivern McGrann McGwin McIllenden McKee McKenna McKeown McLeary McMahon McQuade McShane Montgomery Moore Morrow Mulholland Murphy

Nugent O'Brien O'Hanlon Oliver O'Neil O'Neill Quinn Reynolds Rogers Shields Simpson Slattery Smith Smyth Spence Taggart Taylor Toner Traynor Vallely Ward Wilson Winters Woods

County Carlow

0.8% of our reader's ancestors came from County Carlow. The county had a population of 86,000 in 1841. This had declined to

33,000 by 1961.

Carlow town was once the capital of Ireland. A small, but varied, landlocked county. Here are the names submitted by our readers for County Carlow—they believe that their ancestors lived in this county before emigration:

Alpin Bambrick Brahan Brooks Burton Butler Condren Connolly Denieffe Doyle Edwards Finn Flood Gorman Griffin Hayes Hoare Hogan Joyce Kealy Kelly Keppel Kirwan Lyons MacDonald McGraw Moran Murphy Noctor Nolan Nowlan Nowlin O'Byrne O'Shaugnessy Ryan Smith Tracey Walsh Ward

County Cavan

2.5% of our reader's ancestors came from County Cavan. The county had a population of 243,000 in 1841. This had declined to 57,000 by 1961.

Here are the names submitted by our readers for County Cavan—they believe that their ancestors lived in this county before emigration:

Argue Armstrong Baron Biggins Boylan Bradley Brady Brown Brownlee Campbell Carr Clark Cleary Clerkin Conaty Cosgrove Curran Dale Denning Dolan Doonan Doyle Farrelly Fitzpatrick Fitzsimmons Flannagan Flood

Gaffney Gargan Gavin Gillick Gilsenan Gordon Gourley Greene Halton Hand Hanna Havey Heaslip Hill Hovey Hughes Jamison Kelly Kenny Kernan Kerrigan Kiernan Lally Lamison Lawlers Leddy Lynch

Maguire Masterson McBrien McCabe McCaulay McConnon McCullough McCully McDermott McDonald McDonnell McElroy

McEvoy McGahern McGillick McGinn McGovern McGuigan McHugh McMahan McMahon McMinn McNally Mitchell Murtagh Newell North O'Hara O'Reilly O'Rielly Patterson Poague Pogue Quinn Reilly Reynolds Rielly Rogers Roundtry Scott Seefin Sheridan Smith Smyth Soden Sorohan Sullivan Thompson Trotter Tubman Tweedy Varley Weir Winn

County Clare

5.7% of our reader's ancestors came from County Clare. The county had a population of 286,000 in 1841. This had declined to 74,000 by 1961.

Here are the names submitted by our readers for County Clare—they believe that their ancestors lived in this county before emigration:

Ahern Barrett Belsher Blake Boland Brady Bransfield Brennan Brew Burke Burnell Burns Byrne Cahill Carey Carmody Carrig Casey Clancy Clare Clune Cody Collins Connell Connelly Connole Connors Conoulty Considine Conway Corry Coughlan Coyle Cregan Crotty Crowe Crowley Cunningham Curry Cusack

D'Arcy Davoren Deegan Delahunty Dempsey Dillon Diskin Doherty Donnellan Donohoe Donohue Dooley Downes Doyle Driscoll Dugan Dunleavy Egan Ennis Eustace Fahey Falvey Fennell Fitzgerald Fitzgibbon Fitzmartin Fitzpatrick Flaherty Flanagan Flannagan Foley Foran Fox

Galvin Garvey Geoghegan Gill Glennon Gordon Gorman Gregg Griffin Guinane Gulligan Hall Halloran Hannon Hanrahan haren Harkin Hart Hartigan Haugh Hayes Heffernan Hehir Hennessy Hickey Higgins Hinchy Hogan Hogg Holland Horan Houlihan Howard Hurley Hurst

Keane Keating Kelleher Kelly Keniry Kenneally Kennedy Kiely Kierce Killeen Lacey Langan Larkin Lawler Lawlers Leyden Lillis Linnane Lynch MacDowell MacNamara Madigan Magner Maher Mangan Markham Maroney Marrinan Martell Maxwell Maycock McAllen McDermott McDonnell McEnery McGann McGough McGrath Mcinerney McInerny McKinney McLaughlin McMahon McNamara McNerney McQueeney Meade Melican Minahan Minogue Moloney Morrison Moylan Mulqueen Murphy

Nagle Nash Nelson O'Brian O'Brien O'Bryan O'Connell O'Connor O'Dea O'Donnell O'Grady O'Halloran O'Heffernan O'Keefe O'Loughlin O'Mealy O'Neill O'Shea O'Sullivan Petty Pilkington Quilty Quinlan Quinn Reidy Reynolds Riedy Roach Rogers Rourke Rowan Russell Ryan Scales Scanlan Scanlon Scully Sexton Shalloe Shannon Shaughnessy Sheedy Slattery Sullivan Talty Tierney Tuberty Tubridy Tuohy Waters Welsh Whelan Whyte

County Cork

15.6% of our reader's ancestors came from County Cork. The county had a population of 854,000 in 1841. This had declined to 330,000 by 1961.

Here are the names submitted by our readers for County Cork—they believe that their ancestors lived in this county before emigration:

Abernathy Agger Ahearn Aheren Ahern Allen Arundel Barker Barr Barrett Barron Barry Bartley Beatty Bergen Berry Bluitt Bolger Brady Brannelly Bransfield Brennan Brickley Brislane Brogan Brooks Brophy Brown Browne Buckley Bulman Burdin Burke Butler Byrd Byrnes

Cahill Cain Callaghan Callahan Callanan Camier Cantey Carey

Carmody Carrigan Carroll Carter Case Casey Cashin Cashman Cassidy Cavanaugh Clancy Clarke Cleary Cleland Clifford Clifton Coakley Coffee Coffey Colbert Coleman Collins Collumb Comerford Condon Connally Connell Connery Connolly Connor/Connors Conroy Conway Coogan Coppinger Corbett Corcoran Cork Corkery Corridan Costigan Cotter Cottom Coughlan Coughlin County Coyle Coyne Craddock Crawford Creeden Cremin Cronin Crossen Crowe Crowley Crowly Cullen Culliton Cummings Cunningham Curran Curtin Curtis Cushin

Dabney Daly Daugherty Davis Delaney Deneen Denevan Dennehy Dennison Desmond Deveney Dinan Dineen Dinneen Doheny Donahoe Donahue Donavan Doney Donohue Donovan Dorgan Doyle Drew Driscoll Drummy Duffy Dugan Duggan Dunn Dunnigan Dwyer Dykes

Early Eckley Egan Ellis Ennis Enright Fane Farmer Farrell Fegan Ferdinand Ferrigan Finn Fitzgerald Fitzpatrick Flaherty Flanagan Fleming Fletcher Foley Forrest Fox Freeman Gaffney Gallagher Galligan Galvin Galway Garde Gaughan Geany Geary Gerrity Gibbons Gibson Gill Gilleran Gilman Glatt Glavin Goggin Goulden Green Greer Griffin Grogan

Haggerty Haines Haley Hallahan Haloran Haney Hanlon Harley Harney Harrington Harris Hartigan Hartney Hawk Hawkes Hayes Healey Healy Heard Heffernan Hegarty Hennessey Hennessy Herlihy Hickey Hobbs Hogan Holland Holohan Horgan Hourihan Hourihane Howard Huey Hurley Irish

Jeffers Jeffrey Jennings Joyce Joynt Kanaly Kearney Keefe Kelleher Kelley Kelly Kennedy Kenny Keohane Kieley Kiely Kiley King Kingston Kingstone Kirk Lalley Lamey Land Landers Lane Lawless Leach Leahy Lee Lenihan Leyhane Long Looney Lordan Lucey Luddy Lynch Lyons

MacAuliffe MacDonald Madden Maher Mahoney Mallon Malone Maloney Manning Mannix Marnell Martin Mason McAninley McCall McCann McCarthy McCartney McCarty McCloskey McCormick McCotter McDermott McDevitt McGarry McGill McGinn McGinnis McGlynn McGourn McGrath McGraw McIntyre McKenzie McLaughlin McMahon McSweeney

Meehan Mehegan Mohally Molloy Moran Morey Morrissey Moynahan Mulcahy Mulchinaugh Mulchinock Mullarkey Mullen Mullins Munday Murphy Murray Nally Neely Neenan Neill Newman Nicholson Noonan Nugent

O'Brian O'Brien O'Bryan O'Callaghan O'Colmain O'Connell O'Conner O'Connor O'Cronin O'Donnell O'Donnovan O'Donoghue O'Donovan O'Driscoll O'Flaherty O'Flynn O'Halloran O'Hearn O'Herrons O'Kane O'Keefe O'Keeffe O'Lalley O'Larkin O'Leary O'Mahony O'Malley O'Neil O'Neill O'Niell O'Rourke O'Shaughnessy O'Shea O'Sullivan O'Tuama

Parker Pension Phelan Phillips Philpott Pomeroy Power Powers Poythrus Price Purvis Quill Quinlan Quinn Quirk Raymond Reardon Regan Riley Riordan Roach Roche Rogers Ryan Rylee

Saunders Savage Scanlan Scanlon Shea Shearin Sheehan Sheehy Shine Shinnick Simpson Sisk Slattery Smith Snee Somers Spillane Stanton Stapleton Steele Stewart Stone Sullivan Supple Sutton Sweeney Synge Taylor Terry Thomas Timmons Tobin Toohy Tooker Toomey Tracey Traynor Tuckey Walsh Ward Waters Webb Welch Wells Welsh Weston Whalen White Wholey Winters

County Derry

1.5% of our reader's ancestors came from County Derry. The county had a population of 222,000 in 1841. This had declined to

165,000 by 1961.

Here are the names submitted by our readers for County Derry—they believe that their ancestors lived in this county before emigration:

Atkinson Baird Barnett Bateson Bean Beaston Beatson Boyce Boyd Braden Bradley Breen Caldwell Cassidy Cowan Coyle Creighton Crow Cunningham Curran Dicky Dinsmore Doherty Dougan Duddy Duncan Earle Elliott Fleming Fulton Gannon Gillihan Glenn Guthry

Haggerty Hasson Heaney Hesson Houston Irwin Johnston Kiernan Knox Lamberton Lappin Laughlin Law Lyttle Mallon McCarron McCartney McCashion McCloskey McCluskey McConnell McDevitt McElvaney McKay McKenna McKinnon McLaughlin McLeay McMillan McNeil McNulty McPeake McQuade McQueary McTaggart Miller Molloy Moody Mooney O'Brallaghan O'Cain O'Connor O'Doherty O'Kane Powers Reily Roan Rodgers Smith Strain Sweeney Teague Toughill Toye Vance Warke Whistle

County Donegal

5.6% of our reader's ancestors came from County Donegal. The county had a population of 296,000 in 1841. This had declined to 114,000 by 1961.

Here are the names submitted by our readers for County Donegal—they believe that their ancestors lived in this county before emigration:

Barr Baskin Begley Bonar Boner Bonner Boyce Boyd Boyle Bradley Brennan Breslin Brown Bryson Burke Burns Byrne Canning Cannon Carey Clark Cole Coll Collins Conwell

Corrigan Coyle Crampsey Crawley Daly Daugherty Davis Deery Dever Devlin Diver Docherty Doherty Dolly Donaghy Donahue Donohue Doohan Doonan Doran Doroity Dorrian Dougherty Duffy Dunaway Dunn

Early Elliott Erskine Ewing Flaherty Flanagan Friel Gallagher Gavigan Gill Gillen Gillespie Granahan Grant Haggerty Hamill Hanlon Hannigan Harkin Harkins Harley Hegarty Heraghty Houstin James Kane Kearney Keaveney Kee Keeney Kelly Kerr Kerrigan Kincaid Kirk Knee

Long Lowery Mangin Margey Marshall McAteer McAuley McBrearty McBride McCafferty McCague McCahill McCallion McCann McCarrig McCarron McClafferty McClelland McCloskey McClure McCole McConaha McConnell McCool McDaid McDevitt McDowell McElwaine McFadden McFaul McGarry McGarvey McGee McGeever McGeoghegan McGeoghgan

McGettigan McGill McGinley McGinty McGlinchey McGlynn McGonagle McGonigal McGough McGovern McGowan McGregor McGuinness McHugh McIlhaney McIllwee McIlwain McIntyre McLaughlin McNamee McNelis McPheely Meehan Melley Milligan Molloy Monahan Mooney Morrison Mulhern Mullin Mullins Murray Norfolk

O'Boyle O'Brien O'Cannon O'Doherty O'Donnell O'Hare Orr Orrick Patterson Pettigrew Porter Quigg Quinn Rea Redden Reilly Robinson Rodden Roerty Ryan Scanlon Sharkey Sheedy Sheils Shovlin Simpson Spence Stuart Sweeney Tinney Toland Walsh Weir Wilson Wylie

County Down

2.9% of our reader's ancestors came from County Down. The

county had a population of 361,000 in 1841. This had declined to 267,000 by 1961 (I included the County Borough of Belfast under County Antrim).

Here are the names submitted by our readers for County Down—they believe that their ancestors lived in this county before emigration:

Ardery Bailey Bannon Bell Belshaw Bigham Bingham Binsely Blaney Boyd Brennan Breslin Budd Burns Byrnes Cahill Carmichael Clendenen Collins Connors Corcoran Coulter Crangle Cunningham Dargan Darraugh Daury Dawson DeLargy Denvir Devine Diamond Donley Dorrian Dorris Dougan Downey Drake Duffy

Edgar Fagan Ferguson Ferris Fitzsimmons Fox Garvin Gibson Gilbert Gilbow Gilliland Gilmore Grace Graham Green Gregg Gribbin Gunning Halpin Hamilton Hanvey Heaney Heenan Henneddy Jennings Jess Jordan Kelly Kenealy Kennedy Kielty Laverty Logan Lundy Lyttle

MacMillan Magennis Magenty Maguire Mannis Martin McAlee McCafferty McCartan McCliment McClurg McConnell McCosh McCullough McErlean McGrattan McGuffin McGuinness McKee McKeown McKinney McMillan McMullen McNamara McNeigght McRobert McRoberts McVey Miller Mills Monaghan Moorheads Mulhall Mulholland Mulloy Murphy Murray Nelson O'Neil O'Rourke Osbourne Peters Polley Priestley Quinn Robinson Rooney Rossbotham Ryan Savage Scott Shea Skinner Sloan Smith Smyth Speers Spiby Thompson Todd Tormey Trainor Tremere Turner Wallace Weir Williamson Wright

County Dublin

2.8% of our reader's ancestors came from County Dublin. The county had a population of 372,000 in 1841. This had increased to 718,000 by 1961. Dublin city saw a huge amount of inward migration from the countryside over this time. As a result, many Irish surnames are most numerous today in the Capital city as opposed to their original territory.

Here are the names submitted by our readers for County Dublin—they believe that their ancestors lived in this county before emigration:

Adkins Bannan Bennett Brandon Brennan Burke Byrne Callaghan Carson Caviston Clarke Coffeen Coffey Coleman Comerford Condern Connor Cooke Corcoran Corp Cotter Coyle Crippen Cummins Cunningham Davis Delanny Dixon Donaldson Donlan Doolan Dowling Doyle Dudgen Duffee Dunn Dunphy

Egan English Eslin Evans Faughan Fenlon Free Fulton Gannon Gilligan Grant Gray Halpin Hannah Harford Harper Hawkins Hayde Heffernan Higgins Holmes Hughes Hunt Ireland Iveagh Jennings Jordan Kane Kavanagh Kearney Kearns Kelley Kelly Lalor Leahy Leonard Lyons

Mackey Madden Maloney Mangan Masterson Mc Mahan McAllister McBride McClelland McConnell McGrath McGuire McIntyre McMahon McVickar Mitchell Molloy Monks Mooney Moore Nolan O'Callaghan O'Connely O'Connor O'Flanagan O'Leary O'Neill O'Reilly O'Rourke Osborne Owens Paddock Pollock Puzzau Quinn Redmond Reid Reilly Renshaw Riddell Riley Rolston Ross Ryan Seaver Sharkey Short Shortte Smith Sutton Taylor Tyndall Walsh White Woodard Woods Wright Yeates

County Fermanagh

1.9% of our reader's ancestors came from County Fermanagh. The county had a population of 156,000 in 1841. This had declined to 52,000 by 1961.

Here are the names submitted by our readers for County Fermanagh—they believe that their ancestors lived in this county before emigration:

Amy Armstrong Averell Baxter Beacom Beatty Bevis Bird Booth Brady Carleton Cashon Cassidy Clark Collum Corrigan Creighton Dolan Donaldson Donnelly Dowd English Fair Farrell Fisher Flanagan Gallogly Gillogly Goodwin Graham Green Gunn

Harman Haughy Hicks Huey Johnston Jones Kenney Lafferty Largy Logan Loughnane Lunney Maguire Malloy Maze McBrien McCabe McCauley McCusker McFadden McGee McGhee McGillen McGinn McGrice McGuigan McGuinnis McGuire McLaughlin McManus McVeigh Meehan Moneypenny Moore Moroney Morris Munday Murphy Murray Nugent Peters Quaid Rennick Rowan Slavin Taylor Thompson Tierney Timoney Vance

County Galway

5.3% of our reader's ancestors came from County Galway. The county had a population of 440,000 in 1841. This had declined to 149,000 by 1961.

Here are the names submitted by our readers for County Galway—they believe that their ancestors lived in this county before emigration:

Abberton Athey Balun Barrett Beatty Beegan Blake Brennan Broderick Burke Byrne Cady Cahill Canavan Carr Carroll Carty

Casey Cawley Charlton Cleary Cloonan Coffey Collins Comer Conheeney Conneely Connelly Connolly Connor Conroy Corless Corr Costello Coyne Crowe Cubbard Cullinane Cunniffe Curran Cusack

Davin Dean Deely Dillon Dinan Doherty Dolan Donahoe Donahue Donnellon Donohue Dorsey Dowd Duffy Dugan Egan Fahey Fahy Fair Feeney Fell Finn Finnerty Fitzgerald Flaherty Flannery Fleming Flynn Folan Foley Fox French Gallagher Garvey Gavin Geoghegan Geraghty Gibson Gill Glynn Gordon Gorham Gormley Grealish Guy

Halloran Hannan Hannon Haverty Heanue Hession Hevican Higgins Hobin Hogan Holland Holleran Holmes Horan Hughes Hushion Hynes Irvine Jennings Joyce Keady Kean Keaney Kelley Kelly Kelton Kennedy Kenny Kern Kerwin Kileen Kilkelly King Kirrane Laffey Lardner Lavelle Lee Leech Leonard Linnane Lowery Lunch Lynch Lynskey Lyons

Machan Madden Mahan Malloy Maloney Manion Manning Mannion Martin McAndrew McDonough McDonoughan McHugh McKeever McLaughlin McNalley Melia Mellody Melody Mitchel Molloy Monahan Mongan Mooney Moore Moriarty Morris Morrison Mullaney Mullen Murphy Murray Nall Nee Nelly Noonans Noone Norton

O'Brien O'Connoly O'Dea O'Donnell O'Flaherty O'Halloran O'Loughlin O'Malley O'Shaughnessy O'Toole Pike Quinn Raftery Reardon Regan Ridge Rielly Rooney Ruane Rush Ryan Scarry Screen Scuffle Shehey Skeritt Slowe Smyth Spellman Stanton Stephens Sweeney Tivenan Treacy Walsh Warren Whelan Whyte Sloan

County Kerry

5.5% of our reader's ancestors came from County Kerry. The county had a population of 293,000 in 1841. This had declined to 116,000 by 1961.

Here are the names submitted by our readers for County Kerry—they believe that their ancestors lived in this county before emigration:

Ashe Blennerhasset Bowler Brassil Breen Brennan Brogan Brosnan Browne Burns Cahill Caldwell Callaghan Cannon Carmody Carroll Casey Childerhouse Clifford Coffey Collins Connell Connolly Corcoran Costello Cotter Coughlan Counihan Courtney Crimmins Cronin Curran Cusack

Daly Daugherty Deady DeCourcey Degnan Devlin Dillon Dinneen Dodd Doherty Donnelly Donohue Donovan Doona Dowd Dowling Downey Doyle Duggan Eaton Egan Ferriter Finn Finnegan Fitzgerald Fleming Foley Gallivan Galvin Gamble Garvey Gear Godfrey Goggins Grady Greany Griffin Grogan

Hallissey Halloran Hanafin Harper Hartnett Healy Herlihy Hevican Higgins Hoare Hobert Hogan Holden Hoolihan Humenick Hurley Hussey Keane Kearney Kelleher Kelliher Kelly Keyes Kirby Ladden Landers Lawlor Leahy Leary Long Looney Lovett Lowe Lynch Lyne Lynes

Mack MacMahon Mahoney Mahony Manning Martin Mason McCarthy McCarty McCudden McDonald McDonnell McElligot McGillicuddy McKenna McMahon McSweeney Millane Moore Moriarty Morierty Moynihan Mulchinock Murphy Nolan

O'Connell O'Connor O'Donnell O'Flaherty O'Houlihan O'Leary O'Mara O'Meara O'Neil O'Neill O'Shea O'Sullivan Parker

Purcell Quigley Quill Quilter Quinn Rahilly Reagan Reidy Riney Riordan Roche Rourke Scanlon Scannell Shea Sheehan Sheehy Shine Slattery Spillane Spring Stack Stevens Stratton Sugrue Sullivan Tangney Tempe Walsh Warren Webb White Williams Wonderley Ferris Paine

County Kildare

0.8% of our reader's ancestors came from County Kildare. The county had a population of 114,000 in 1841. This had declined to 64,000 by 1961.

Here are the names submitted by our readers for County Kildare—they believe that their ancestor lived in this county before emigration:

Bolger Brady Bryan Burke Campbell Carney Carroll Connoly Craddock Cuff Deegan Fitzgerald Flannagan Garland Goucher Graham Hannon Hayde Ingram Kerr Lehane Leonard Lewis Marsh McCormack Mills Moran Muldowney Mulhall Murphy Payne Reed Roantree Ryan Stewart Tighe Walsh O'Nolan

County Kilkenny

2.3% of our reader's ancestors came from County Kilkenny. The county had a population of 202,000 in 1841. This had declined to 61,000 by 1961.

Here are the names submitted by our readers for County Kilkenny—they believe that their ancestors lived in this county before emigration:

Anderson Archdeacon Bearer Berrigan Boran Bowe Brannen

Brennan Brett Brophy Burns Butler Byrne Byrnes Cahill Campbell Cantwell Carey Clancy Coady Cody Collings Collins Connor Connors Conway Cormac Costello Cove Croke Cronyn Crow Cuddihy Deady Delaney Dempsey Denieffe Dermody Dillon Dooley Dowling Dungan Dunn Dwan Fennelly Ferguson Fitzpatrick Fitzsimons Fogarty Galvin Gannon Gorman Griffin Grogan Guilfoyle

Hamilton Hanrahan Hawe Healy Heffernan Hickey Hoban Holahan Holly Hunt Hurley Irish Ivory Kearney Keefe Kelly Kennedy Keogh Kirwin Lahey Lyng Lyons Maher McCartan McGuire McLaughlin Morressy Morris Muldowney Murphy Murray Naughton O'Braonain O'Brien O'Connell O'Donnell O'Leary O'Mara O'Shea O'Stahl Phelan Pielow Plunkett Power Purcell Rafter Reade Roche Ryan Sansburn Sheehan Sheridan Shortall Sullivan Sweeney Walsh Walton Welch

County Laois

0.9% of our reader's ancestors came from County Laois. The county had a population of 153,000 in 1841. This had declined to 45,000 by 1961.

Here are the names submitted by our readers for County Laois—they believe that their ancestors lived in this county before emigration:

Aiken Barnett Bergin Brophy Carter Cavanaugh Chambers Clooney Cranney Dempsey Dowling Doyle Dunne Fahey Feeney Finn Fitzgerald Fitzpatrick Fleming Goss Hayes Heffernan Hetherington Keating Kelly Langford Lawler Lovette McDermott McDonald McEvoy McLean Moore Morrisey Mulhall Nolan O'Connor O'Dea Rudd Scott Scully Tobin Wall White Wilson

Wright

County Leitrim

1.7% of our reader's ancestors came from County Leitrim. The county had a population of 155,000 in 1841. This had declined to 33,000 by 1961.

Here are the names submitted by our readers for County Leitrim—they believe that their ancestors lived in this county before emigration:

Byrne Campbell Carrigan Casey Clarke Conroy Corcoran Costello Cullen Cunningham Darcy Dinnen Dorigan Dunne Faughnan Flynn Fowley Fox Gallagher Gilbride Gilmartin Gormley Green Grennan Hannon Heeran Higgins Keeran Kelly Kennedy Kiernan Leathong Lenihan

Mahan Mahon Marlowe McCartin McCue McGarry McGoey McGoldrick McGoohan McGowan McGrail McGuire McGurn McKeon McKiernan McNulty McPartlan McSharry McTiernan McTigue Mostyn Mulligan Mulvey Murray Myers Noone O'Hara O'Neil O'Rourke Rahal Reilly Reynolds Richards Roark Roarke Shanley Shaw Smyth Stretton Tiernan Travers Walsh White

County Limerick

3.3% of our reader's ancestors came from County Limerick. The county had a population of 330,000 in 1841. This had declined to 133,000 by 1961.

Here are the names submitted by our readers for County Limerick—they believe that their ancestors lived in this county before emigration:

Bagnall Barry Barton Bluett Bourke Bovenizer Bowen Boyle Brigman Brown Burke Byron Cahill Carmody Carroll Carrolls Caswell Chamber Childerhouse Cleary Clifford Coleman Collins Collopy Colwell Connors Conway Copps Cottom Coughlin Cronin Culhane Cullen Cunneen Cussen Daly Davern Dempsey Doneen Doran Dowd Downes Doyle Dunne

Ennalls Enright Falahee Farrell Finn Fitzgerald Fitzgibbon Flaherty Flynn Fogarty Gainey Gaynor Geary Gernon Gillespie Gillon Gleeson Glenney Griffith Hannan Hannon Harold Hartigan Hassett Hayes Hays Healey Heffernan Hennessy Herbert Hickey Hinchy Hogan Hourigan Howey Hurley Ivers Keane Keane Keating Kelly Kinnerk Kirwan Lacey Lacy Lawler Leakey Liston Lynch Madigan Maher Mahoney Maunsell McCarthy McCormack McCurren McDonall McGrath McMahan McQueen Mee Minihan Minnehan Molohon Mortell Mulcahy Murphy

Nash Naughton Nealon Neville Nichols Nihill Nolan O'Connell O'Connor O'Donnell O'Donoghue O'Heffernan O'Regan O'Rourke O'Shaughnessy O'Shea O'Sullivan Quinn Raynard Ready Real Reidy Ring Riordan Ryan Sexton Shanahan Sheedy Sheehan Shier Smyth Spelessy Spillane Switzer Teskey Tobin Toomey Tracey Trawley Vassey Wade Walsh Watson Welsh Woulfe

County Longford

1.2% of our reader's ancestors came from County Longford. The county had a population of 115,000 in 1841. This had declined to 31,000 by 1961.

Here are the names submitted by our readers for County Longford—they believe that their ancestors lived in this county before emigration:

Connaughton Adams Ahern Blake Brady Campbell Columb Corrigan Cullinan Dimond Duffy Duignan Fallon Farrell Ferrell Finsely Ginty Heaney Johnston Kane Keane Keating Kelly Kidney Killian Larkin Lennon Loftus Lynch McCabe McCauley McClaughry McCreanor McDermott McGann McGovern McKenna Mulligan Mulvihill Murray Murtha Nulty O'Farrell Quinn Radigan Rawl Reilly Rodgers Rudden Seery Shanley Shannon Smith Walsh Whitney York

County Louth

0.8% of our reader's ancestors came from County Louth. The county had a population of 128,000 in 1841. This had declined to 67,000 by 1961.

Here are the names submitted by our readers for County Louth—they believe that their ancestors lived in this county before emigration:

Brannon Breagy Byrne Callan Carroll Cassidy Clarke Clerk Connolly Curran Devine Doyle Duffy Finegan Harmon Kavanagh Kelledy Levins Lynch Mathews McCabe McDonald McDonough McKeon Moyles Mulholland Murphy Newcomb O'Hara Pentony Rafferty Reilly Reynolds Rogan Rooney Shane Short Simpson Taaffe Trotter Venable Yore

County Mayo

9.1% of our reader's ancestors came from County Mayo. The county had a population of 388,000 in 1841. This had declined to 123,000 by 1961.

Here are the names submitted by our readers for County Mayo—they believe that their ancestors lived in this county before emigration:

Ansbro Bailey Barrett Beatty Begley Beirne Bermingham Bird Blackburn Bloxham Bourke Boylan Boyle Brannick Brennan Breslin Brett Browne Burke Burns Butler Byrne Cadden Cafferty Caine Cairns Callaghan Canavan Cannon Carben Carey Carlin Carney Carolan Casey Cassidy Caufield Caulfield Chambers Clarke Coleman Collins Conlon Conners Connolly Connor Conroy Conway Cooney Costello Coughlin Coyle Coyne Craven Crean Cuff Culbreath Cullina Cummings Cunnane Cunningham

Daly Dane Davies Davitt Devanney Dever Devlin Devor Dixon Doherty Dolan Donlon Donnelly Dougherty Dowd Duffy Dulin Dunleavy Durcan Durkan Durkin Eagney Earley Early Fallon Farragher Fee Feeley Feerick Fergus Finn Fitzmaurice Fitzpatrick Flanagan Flannigan Flatley Flynn Ford Forry Forster Foster Foy Frain Freeley Freil Friel Gallagher Galvin Ganley Gannon Garrey Garry Garvey Garvin Gaughan Gavaghan Gavin Geraghty Gibbons Gilmartin Gormley Gough Grady Granahan Graney Greeley Greely

Hall Halligan Hanahan Haney Harrington Hart Hastings Haugh Healey Healy Henaughan Heneghan Henehan Henry Hickey Higgins Hoban Hogan Hope Huane Hughes Hurst Hyland Hynes Igoe Jordan Joyce Judge Kane Kavanagh Keady Keane Kearns Keenan Kelly Kennedy Kenny Kerins Kerrigan Kilbane Kilbride Kilcoyne Kilgallon Kilgariff Kilroy Kneafsey Lally Landers Larrisey Lavelle Layng Leonard Levy Linsky Loftus Ludden Lyden Lydon Lynagh Lynch Lynskey

Madden Malley Malloney Malone Maloney Marney McAndrew McBride McCauley McDermot McDonagh McDonald McDonnell McEvey McEvoy McGibbon McGinty McGowan McGrayel

McGreal McGuigan McGuinn McGuire McHale McHugh McLauchlan McLaughlin McManus McMenamin McMonagle McNamara McNeice McNicholas McNulty McQuaide McTigue McVady Mealey Millet Minoughan Molloy Monahan Monnelly Moore Moran Morley Morrison Morrisson Mortimer Muldowney Mullaney Mullen Mulligan Mulroy Munley Munnelly Murphy Murray Naughton Nealon Neary Nellany Nolan Noone

O'Boyle O'Brien O'Connor O'Donnell O'Gara O'Hale O'Hara O'Hora O'Mailia O'Malley O'Rourke O'Sullivan O'Toole Owens Padden Parker Patterson Payne Phillips Plover Prendergast Pue Pugh Quinn Rabbit Radigan Rainey Reaney Regan Riley Roach Rooney Ruane Rush Ryan Sands Scully Sheeran Sheerin Sheridan Sherrans Smith Stenson Sweeney Swift Tarpey Tighe Tolan Tonra Toole Totton Treacy Tucker Tully Tunney Turbett Vahey Waldron Walsh Walton Webb Williams

County Meath

1.2% of our reader's ancestors came from County Meath. The county had a population of 183,000 in 1841. This had declined to 65,000 by 1961.

Here are the names submitted by our readers for County Meath—they believe that their ancestors lived in this county before emigration:

Bannen Barry Butler Byrnes Cassidy Clark Clinch Conner Cummiskey Dillon Dolan Durgy Farrell Fields Finnegan Fitzsimmons Fitzsimons Flannigan Foley Foy Giblin Gillick Gilsenan Goodwin Growney Halpin Heary Hogan Hughes Kangley Keeran Kennedy King

Lane Leonard Lowther Lynam Lynch Mahon Malone McCann

McDonnell McFarren McGrane McLaughlin McMahon McNally McNamee Meeke Monahan Mooney Murphy Murray Nangle Netterville O'Daly Parker Pender Reilly Riley Rispin Shanley SheehySmith Tully Williams Yore Manning

County Monaghan

1.4% of our reader's ancestors came from County Monaghan. The county had a population of 200,000 in 1841. This had declined to 47,000 by 1961.

Here are the names submitted by our readers for County Monaghan—they believe that their ancestors lived in this county before emigration:

Bowes Boyd Brannigan Brown Callan Carolan Carragher Carroll Cassidy Conally Connolly Deering Duffy Duggan Durnin Eager Faulkner Fawcett Fields Finnegan Fitzpatrick Gauley Halfpenny Hughes Karr Keenan Kellegher Kelly Larkin Lillis Lynn

MacPhillips Maguire Malone Martin McCabe McCarney McCarron McCaul McConnon McCudden McFarlane McGeough McGuinness McKay McKeague McKee McKeever McKenna McKittricks McMahon McQuade Meehan Moor Moorhead Morris Murray Quigley Quinn Sheridan Smyth Stephens SuitorTaggart Timmins Trainor Treanor Ward Waters Weir Wiggins

County Offaly

0.9% of our reader's ancestors came from County Offaly. The county had a population of 147,000 in 1841. This had declined to 52,000 by 1961.

Here are the names submitted by our readers for County Offaly—they believe that their ancestors lived in this county before emigration:

Carroll Coleman Connolly Corcoran Culgin Cullen Dempsey Dooley Dunne Dunns Egan Flannagan Flynn Hogan Hyland Keenahan Kelly Lane Loney Malloy McMahon Menton Mooney Moran Moren Mullally Murphy Murray O'Bannon O'Bannion O'Carrol O'Connor O'Madden O'Reilly Rafter Rigney Smith Smyth Stone Warren Watson Yeats

County Roscommon

2.5% of our reader's ancestors came from County Roscommon. The county had a population of 254,000 in 1841. This had declined to 59,000 by 1961.

Here are the names submitted by our readers for County Roscommon—they believe that their ancestors lived in this county before emigration:

Beades Beirne Brehon Brennan Bresnahan Burke Butler Byrne Byron Casey Cassidy Cawley Charley Coady Collins Conaughton Conlin Connaughton Connor Cox Coyne Crawford Croughan Cunniff Cunningham Curley D'Arcy Deffley Diffley Dillon Donoghue Doyle Egan Fallon Feeley Fetherston Filan Finan Finerty Finnegan Finnerty Flanagan Flynn Gaffin Garrity Giblin Giblins Gilmartin Gilooly Gilrain Glancy Glennon Glynn Gonoude Grace Grinham

Hanley Hayden Healy Heffernan Hevican Higgins Hoar Hogarty Horan Kaveny Keane Keegan Keena Keigher Kelly Kenny Killelea Kimmet Lane Larkin Leonard Lynch Lyons Martin Mauriceroe McDermott McGaughan McGee McHugh McLoughlin McManus

McNulty Moore Mosgrove Mulrenan Murphy Murray Murtagh Neilan O'Brien O'Connor O'Gara Padian Quinn Radigan Reddy Reynolds Rush Savage Shanahan Shannon Sheeran Sheerin Skeffington Smith Sullivan Surlis Tague Thullis Tiernan Webb Winston

County Sligo

2.6% of our reader's ancestors came from County Sligo. The county had a population of 180,000 in 1841. This had declined to 54,000 by 1961.

Here are the names submitted by our readers for County Sligo—they believe that their ancestors lived in this county before emigration:

Armstrong Auliff Banks Barber Beatty Brennan Cahill Canty Carbury Casey Cawley Clark Clarke Coleman Colman Coyle Cuffe Culleens Cullen Cummiskey Cunningham Currid Daly Donegan Doyle Drury Dunigan Durcan Durkin Dyer Fahey Farrell Fee Feeley Feeney Finan Finnigan Flannery Flynn Foley Gallagher Gardiner Gartland Geary Gilgan Gillespie Gilmartin Gilmore Grady Graham Hawkins Healy Henry Herly Higgins Hunt Jennings Jinks Jordan Judge

Kelly Kennedy Kenney Kerrigan Kilcullen Kilroy Lacken Lang Layng Loftus Loughlin Lyons Madden Maguire Malloy Marren McCafferkey McDonough McEttrick McGarry McGary McGloin McGowan McKeon McKeown McTeirnan Meehan Meer Middleton Moore Moriarty Morrison Mulligan Mulvaney Musgrave Niland O'Gara O'Hara O'Neill O'Shea Owens Pugh Quinn Rafferty Regan Scanlon Scott Scully Sharkey St Lawrence Stimson Stinson Sweeney Vesey Walsh White Young

County Tipperary

4.7% of our reader's ancestors came from County Tipperary. The county had a population of 435,000 in 1841. This had declined to 123,000 by 1961.

Here are the names submitted by our readers for County Tipperary—they believe that their ancestors lived in this county before emigration:

Ahern Aylward Bannon Barry Beary Blake Bonney Bourke Bowes Brett Britt Browne Brunnock Bryan Burgess Burke Butler Cahill Cain Carden Carey Carney Carroll Casey Chamberlain Charlton Clancy Cleary Coady Coffey Colue Corbett Costello Costelloe Cotter Coughlin Crotty Culleton Cummings Cummins

Dailey Daley Daly Daven Dempsey Doherty Donahue Donnelly Donovan Dwyer Echlen Eddington Egan Emerson English Fahy Fannons Fennessy Field Fitzgerald Fitzpatrick Floyd Flynn Fogarty Funchion Galligan Gavin Gaynor Geaney Giltinane Gleason Gleeson Gorman Grady Hanley Harrigan Haslett Hawkes Hawkins Hayes Heffernan Hennessy Herrick Hogan Holway Horan Houlihan Hyde Hyland Jackson Kane Kay Keefe Kelleher Kennedy Kenney Keogh King Kirwan Lahy Landers Lanigan Leary Lewis Lloyd Lonergan Long Looby Luby Luttrell Lynch Lyons Mackey Madden Maher Mahoney Maloughny McElliot McEvoy McGrath McNamara Meagher Meara Moloney Monahan Mooney Moore Moran Morrissey Moyles Mulcahy Mullally Murphy Nolan

Oakman O'Bannon O'Brien O'Byrne O'Connor O'Donnell O'Dwyer O'Gorman O'Halloran O'Mara O'Meara O'Neill O'Reilly O'Sullivan Pendergrast Pennefeather Powell Preston Purcell Purtill Quinlan Quinn Rockett Roughan Ryan Shanahan Shea Shelley Slattery Smeltzer Smith Spillane Stanley Talbot Tierney Tobin Torpey Tracy Tucker Tyrrell Vaughan Walsh Webster Wellwood

County Tyrone

2.9% of our reader's ancestors came from County Tyrone. The county had a population of 313,000 in 1841. This had declined to 134,000 by 1961.

Here are the names submitted by our readers for County Tyrone—they believe that their ancestors lived in this county before emigration:

Adams Alexander Anderson Barclay Braden Bradley Bruffey Bryson Buchanan Calderwood Caldwell Calhoun Carlin Carlon Carolin Carson Casey Coffee Collum Corr Courtney Crawford Daley Davey Davis Devlin Dillon Dollis Duff Earley Early Findley Flynn Galeen Galleen Garvin Gibboney Gibson Gilchrist Glennon Gorman Gray Greer Grieves Hackett Hamill Haston Heagney Hempill Hide Hughes Johnston Kelly Kennedy Killeran Lafferty Lambert Latimer Laverty Leonard Logan Logue Loughran Loy

MacAroy MacCartney Macklam MacKnew Mallahan Mallon Martin Maune McAleer McBride McCaffery McCaffrey McCallion McCarron McClanahan McCollum McConaha McCook McCooney McCormick McCracken McCreary McCurdy McCusker McDonald McElhatton McEllhatton McFarland McGarrity McGinley McGlynn McGrath McGuckin McGurren McHugh McKenna McKinney McLaughlin McLean McNulty McSorley Mellon Monaghan Moore Mullen Murphy Murray Neville Nickell

O'Brien O'Donnell O'Hagan O'Neill Orr Paisley Pomeroy Quinn Redmond Rooney Scott Seaton Seawright Seens Shea Shinners Skivington Smyth Smyton Snodgrass Sproul Symington Tassey Thompson Trimble Turbett Turbitt Vaughan Wallace

County Waterford

1.7% of our reader's ancestors came from County Waterford. The county had a population of 196,000 in 1841. This had declined to 71,000 by 1961.

Here are the names submitted by our readers for County Waterford—they believe that their ancestors lived in this county before emigration:

Ahearn Barnidge Beastwick Black Boyle Browner Burns Butler Cantwell Carr Caruth Cleary Clooney Connell Connolly Connory Conway Corcoran Cosgrove Costello Croke Cunningham Daly Davey Egan Evans Finn Flynn Foley Furlong Godfrey Guiry Heffernan Hennebry Hogan Hunt Hurley Keane Keily Kenneally Kenure Kiely Kiley Leckie

Leonard Long Lyons Maher Mahoney Martin McCarthy McGrath Moakler Mohoney Moore Munn Murphy Navin O'Brien Porter Power Powers Regan Roach Roche Roe Shortis Sullivan Supple Synott Terry Wall Walsh Whalen White Whitty

County Westmeath

1.5% of our reader's ancestors came from County Westmeath. The county had a population of 141,000 in 1841. This had declined to 53,000 by 1961.

Here are the names submitted by our readers for County Westmeath—they believe that their ancestors lived in this county before emigration:

Ahearn Bagley Begley Bohan Brady Broder Brougham Byrnes Callaghan Callahan Casey Cashin Coffey Conaty Cormack Coyne Cullen Daley Daly Darcy Delamer Dillon Dooley Dorsey Earley

Evers Fagan Farrell Flynn Foley Gaffney Gallagher Garvey Gavin Geoghan Geraghty Gillick Ginell Gorman Heaney Higgins Jeffries Jeffert

Kearney Kehoe Kenny Kiernan Killoughy Lavin MacGeoghegan MacNamee Mahon Maney Manning Mannion McGuigan Mulhall Murphy Murray Nally Nugent O'Farrell O'Reilly O'RourkeRedden Reilly Rigney Riley Rush Seery Sheehy Stanley Stone Tierney Tormey Tumulty Tyrrell

County Wexford

2.2% of our reader's ancestors came from County Wexford. The county had a population of 202,000 in 1841. This had declined to 83,000 by 1961.

Here are the names submitted by our readers for County Wexford—they believe that their ancestors lived in this county before emigration:

Aspel Berney Bishop Bolger Brett Browne Buggy Bulger Butler Byrne Byrnes Cahill Carroll Casey Cavanaugh Codd Coe Colclough Colfer Corcoran Cox Crosbie Cullen Dempsey Devine Devlin Doyle Edwards Fanning Fardy Fitzgerald Flynn Furlong Gaffney Gahan Gannon Gavin Goff Gunnip Haggerty Hall Hempinstall Hope Howlin Jones

Kanary Kavanagh Kelly Kennedy Kielthy Kinsella Kinsley Kirwan Lacey Lannan Libby Lyng Martyn McDonald McGrievy Molloy Mordaunt Morris Murdoch Murphy Noctor Nolan O'Byrne O'Connor O'Keeffe O'Neill O'Shea Ralph Redmond Roche Rooney Rose Rossiter Rossiters Ryan Sheehan Sinnott Skelton Stanton Stuart Sutton Teague Walsh Whitty

County Wicklow

0.8% of our reader's ancestors came from County Wicklow. The county had a population of 126,000 in 1841. This had declined to 58,000 by 1961.

Here are the names submitted by our readers for County Wicklow—they believe that their ancestors lived in this county before emigration:

Barnes Barry Bates Byrne Byrnes Cavanagh Clarke Coates Critchley Doyle Finley Fitzhenry Gahan Gartland Johnson Jones Kavanagh Keane Keenan Kennedy Keogh McAttackneys McHendrick McQuillan O'Byrne O'Toole Pender Penrose Power Rooney Shannon Toole Turke Twyford Tyrrell Waldron Wall Ward Whelan Whiteacre Yates

Don't Know

Sometimes a reader just does not know which county their Irish ancestor departed from. I have put all those Irish surnames here.

Acheson Adams Adkins Ahern Ahrens Aikens Albree Alcott Alford Allen Ambrose Anderson Andrews Apple Archer Arkwood Armstrong Arrick Atkins

Bagge Baggott Bagley Bailey Baird Baker Baldwin Balfe Ballinger Bambery Barclay Barnes Barnett Baron Barr Barr Barrett Barrie Barron Barry Bartley Barton Beard Beasley Beattie Beatty Beaty Begley Behan Bell Benner Bergin Berrigan Best Birchfield Black Blair Blake Blayney Blee Bogan Bohannon Boland Bolton Bonar Bonds Bonner Borden Bowlen Boyd Boylan Boyle Boylen Boyne Brackney Braddy Braden Bradley Brady Bragg Branigan Brannaugh Brannian Brannigan Brannon Bray Breadin Breanach Breen

Brennan Brent Bresnahan Brett Bride Britton Brock Broderick Brogan Bronson Brooks Brown Brown Bruce Brugh Bryan Bryarly Bryson Buckley Bunn Buntain Burke Burnes Burnim Burns Burrell Burrows Burt Burton Bustard Butler Byrne Byrnes

Cahaney Cahill Cain Calannon Cales Calhoun Callaghan Callahan Callan Callantine Calloway Campbell Canavan Cannon Canovan Capeheart Caplice Carberry Carew Carey Carlen Carlin Carlon Carmichael Carnahan Carney Carolan Caroll Carpenter Carr Carrell Carrig Carroll Carson Carter Casey Cashien Cashman Cassidy Caswell Cavanagh Cavanaugh Caverlee Cawley Chaney Childress Clacherty Claire Clancey Clancy Clannan Clark Clarke Clary Cleary Clifford Clinch Clisdell Clough Coady Coakley Coates Cobey Coburn Cochran Codd Cody Coey Coffey Coleman Coll Colleran Colley Collins Colohan Colvin Combs Comerford Conarton Conaton Conaty Concannon Condon Conerly Conklin Conley Conlin Conlon Conn Connell Connelly Conner Conners Connolly Connor Connors Conroy Conway Cook Cooke Cooley Cooney Cooper Corcoran Corey Corr Corrigan Costello Costelloe Cotter Coughlin Coulter Courtney Cowan Cowley Cox Coxsey Coyne Crahan Craig Crawford Crean Creegan Creelman Cregon Creighton Cremeans Crew Crimmins Crogan Crohan Cronin Crosbie Crosley Crosse Crosset Crow Crowe Crowley Culbertson Cullen Culley Culliton Culpepper Cumberlander Cummings Cummins Cunniff Cunningham Curley Curran Currie Curry Cursey Curtis Cusack Cusick Cuthbert

Dalton Daly Daniel Daniels Dardis Darling Darmody Daugherty Daughty Davey Davidson Davies Davis Dawes Decker Delaney Delay DeLucry Dempsey Denne Dennis Dermody Desmond Devany DeVaugh Devine Devlin Dewhurst Dicks Diffley Dill Dillen Dillon Dillow Dinan Dineen Dingman Dinsmore Diver Dixon Doan Dobson Dodd Doggett Doherty Dolan Donahue Donaldson Donathan Donavan Donelson Donlan Donlon

Donnelly Donovan Donworth Doohan Doolin Doran Doreen Dority Dorris Dorrity Dothard Dougherty Douglas Dowd Dowdy Dowling Downey Downing Doyle Dozer Draper Drennan Driscoll Drohan Duddy Duffer Duffy Duggan Duignan Dunahoe Duncan Dunigan Dunkin Dunleavy Dunlevy Dunn Dunne Dunnigan Dunning Dunworth Durkin Dwan Dwyer Dyer

Eades Eagan Earl Earle Earley Eccles Egan Elliot Ellis Elver Elwood Ennis Enright Erskine Erwin Estridge Evans Everett Eyre Fabish Fahey Fairchild Fales Fallon Fanning Faraher Farley Farr Farrell Farrelly Farris Farson Faulkner Fay Faye Feeley Feeney Fenton Ferguson Ferrel Ferrell Ferris Ferron Ffrench Fields Finley Finn Finnernan Finnerty Finnigan Finnucane Finucane Fisher Fitzgerald Fitzgibbon Fitzpatrick FitzSimmons Flaharty Flaherty Flanagan Flanigan Flannery Flaven Fleming Flemming Flood Flower Floyd Flannery Floyd/Flood Fluharty Flynn Fogarty Foley Foran Ford Forken Fox Foxe Foy Fraley Francis Frayne Frazier Friel Fry Furey Furlong Fyfe

Gage Gahagan Gailey Gallagher Gallaher Gallogly Galloway Gann Gannon Gardner Gartland Garvey Garvin Gaston Gaughan Gavin Gaynor Geary Geer Geoghagen Geoghan Geoghegan George Geraghty Gibbons Gibbs Gibson Gilbride Gill Gillaspie Gillespie Gilley Ginnebaugh Glasscock Glavin Gleason Glencross Glennon Glin Glines Glover Glynn Golden Goode Goodwin Gordon Gorman Gough Gould Goulden Gove Gowin Grady Graham Grahms Graney Grant Gray Greaney Green Greene Greer Gregg Gregory Grey Griffin Griffith Griggs Grimes Grindle Grogan Guilfoyle Guinan Gunning Gwynn

Hackett Hagan Haggan Haggarty Haggerty Hale Haley Hall Halloran Halpin Hamilton Hammond Hana Hanafin Handrahan Haney Hanley Hanlon Hanna Hannan Hanney Hannon Hanrahan Harbison Harden Hare Hargedon Harkin Harkins Harkness

Harney Harper Harrigan Harrington Harris Harrison Harrity Hart
Hartney Harty Harvey Hassett Haverty Hawkins Hay Hayden
Hayes Hays Healey Healy Heaney Hearn Hearst Heath Hedden
Heffernan Heffron Hegarty Hege Henderson Hennedy Hennessy
Hennigan Henry Hepburn Herlihy Herndon Herring Heslin Hester
Hickey Hicks Higgins Hill Hilley Hind Hindman Hines Hinson
Hinton Hobson Hoey Hogan Holder Holland Hollinger Hollon
Holman Hood Hooly Hopkins Horan Horgan Horn Hourigan
Howard Hoyt Huddleston Hudson Huey Hughes Humphrey Hunt
Hunter Hurley Hurst Hussey Hutchinson Hyland Idiens Igoe
Irving Irwin Jackson Jacobs Jameson Jamison Jenkins Jennings
Johnson Johnston Jones Jordan Jordon Joyce

Kane Kavanagh Kealey Kealty Kearney Keating Keaton Keegan
Keeley Keenan Keeney Keerigan Keesey Kegan Kehoe Keleher
Kell Kelleher Keller Kellet Kelley Kells Kelly Kennedy Kennelley
Kenney Kenny Keohane Keough Kernan Kerns Kerr Kiernan
Kilcoyne Killeen Killen Kilraine Kinch Kinnamon Kinney Kinsella
Kirby Kirk Kirkpatrick Kirwin Kissinger Kline Knox Kyle Lacey
Lackey Ladd Laffey Lahart Lahey Laird Lambe Landis Lane
Langan Lappin Larkey Larkin Lasley Laurie Lavender Laverty
Lawler Lawler Lawlor Lawrence Lawton Leahy Leatham Lee
Leeper Lehane Leland Lenahan Lenehan Lennard Lennon Leonard
Lester Lewis Lisco Lloyd Lockhart Loftus Lonergan Long Looney
Loughary Loughman Loughran Lovejoy Lowney Lowrie Lucas
Lyle Lynam Lynch Lyons

Macaulay MacDonald Mace MacElroy MacFarland Mack Mackay
Mackin MacKinney MacMachado MacNamee Madden Madigan
Madole Magacking Magadan Magarvey Magee Magennis Maguire
Mahagan Maher Mahoney Mahony Mahr Malanaphy Malia Malley
Mallon Malloy Malone Maloney Manday Manion Manley Manning
Mannion Mannon Maroney Marshall Martin Mason Matheney
Mathews Matteson Maybury Maynard McAdoo McAfee McAlarney

McAllister McAlpine McAlvey McAndrew McAneny McAninch
McArdle McAteer McAvoy McBee McBeth McBride McCabe
McCafferty McCaffery McCaffrey McCandless McCann McCarl
McCarley McCarrick McCarten McCarthy McCartney McCarty
McCauley McChoney McClafferty McClain McClaran McClean
McCleery McClellan McClement McClendons McClisham
McCloud McClure McCluskey McConnaughey McConnell
McConney McCool McCormack McCormick McCorry McCory
McCourt McCoy McCracken McCray McCrea McCreary
McCrohan McCrory McCrudden McCulley McCullough McCurdy
McCurry McCusker McDaniel McDermott McDonald McDonell
McDonnell McDonough McDormand McDow McDowell
McDuffie McElroy McElwee McEnaney McErlean McEvoy
McFadden McFaddin McFalls McFarland McFee

McGann McGaoulif McGarrity McGarry McGee McGhan
McGhee McGinnis McGinniss McGinnley McGinty McGlaughlin
McGlinn McGlone McGoldrick McGonigal McGovern McGowan
McGrath McGroarty McGuigan McGuin McGuinn McGuire
McHargue McHenry McHugh McIlhaney McElhaney McIlwain
Mcilwee McInerney McInness McIntire McIntosh McIntyre McKay
McKeage McKeating McKee McKelvey McKelvie McKenna
McKeon McKeough McKeown McKey McKim McKinley
McKinna McKinney McKinstry McKinzie McKnight McLain
McLaughlin McLeary McLellen McLennan McLeon McLimans
McLoughlin McMahan McMahon McManegle McManus
McMasters McMenamin McMillan McMillin McMullen McMullin
McMurray McMyler McNabb McNally McNamara McNeely
McNees McNeice McNeil McNeile McNemee McNey McNicholas
McNiff McNulty McNutt McPeters McPhail McPhillips McQuade
McQuality McQuay McQueen McRee McReynolds McShane
McSpedon McTighe McVeen McVey McWeeney McWilliams Mead
Meade Meagher Meehan Mehan Mehegen Merrigan Miles Millen

Miller Milligan Mills Minnis Minsey Mitchell Moates Moffatt Moffet Moffit Molloy Monaghan Monahan Mondy Monk Montgomery Mooney Moore Moran Morey Morgan Moriarty Morning Morris Morrisey Morrison Morrissey Morrow Moss Moyers Moylan Moynihan Muchinoch Mulcahy Mulconery Muldoon Mulhall Mulhearn Mulholland Mullaney Mullarkey Mullen Muller Mullican Mulligan Mullin Mullins Mullooly Mullowney Mulroony Mulvaney Mulvey Mulvihill Mungavin Murdock Murphree Murphy Murray Murtagh Murtha Myers

Nagle Naismith Nash Neal Nealon Neely Neil Nelligan Nelson Nesbitt Nestor Netterville Newell Newmarch Newton Nichol Nichols Nickell Niland Nolan Noonan Normile Norris Nowland Nowlin Nugent Nunan Nunnery

Oates O'Bannon O'Beirne O'Boyle O'Bray O'Brian O'Brien O'Briens O'Bryan O'Calligan O'Carmody O'Carroll O'Cassidy O'Clisham O'Connell O'Conner O'Connor O'Dea O'Dell O'Dempsey O'Doherty O'Donnell O'Donoghoe O'Donoghue O'Dooley O'Dougherty O'Dowd O'Doyle O'Driscoll O'Duggan O'Durgy O'Flaherty O'Flannery O'Flynn O'Gara O'Garr Oglesby O'Gorman O'Grady O'Hagan O'Hannigan O'Hanrahan O'Hara O'Hare O'Higgins O'Hora O'Hoy O'Keefe O'Killea O'Lalley O'Laughlin O'Leary O'Lone O'Loughlin O'Loyal O'Mahony O'Malley O'Meara O'Meehan O'Neal O'Neil O'Neil O'Neill O'Pry O'Reagan O'Regan O'Reilly O'Rielly O'Riley O'Riordan Ormerod Ormsby O'Rourke Orr Osborne O'Shea O'Sorahan O'Sullivan O'Toole Otter Owens

Pace Parke Parker Parnell Patrick Patterson Pattison Patton Paul Payne Peacock Peckham Peel Peevey Pendleton Perkins Perry Peters Pheley Phillips Philpot Picken Pierce Pierson Piper Plunkett Poe Pollock Porter Pouton Powell Powers Predmore Preece Price Prior Pritt Proctno Pruitt Quigley Quilty Quinan Quinley

Quinlivan Quinn Quinton Quirk

Rae Rafferty Rafter Raggett Raher Rahilly Raley Randall Rankin Rea Redding Reddy Redican Redman Redmond Reeve Regan Reid Reilly Reily/Riley Reynolds Rice Riddle Ridgway Rigney Riley Rinney Riordan Rippy Roach Robb Roberts Robinson Roche Roden Rodgers Rogers Rohan Rooney Rorie Rose Rothwell Roundtree Rountree Rourke Routon Rowan Ruane Rudd Rush Russell Ruth Rutherford Rutledge Ryan

Sale Savage Savard Scanlon Scobey Scollon Scott Scully Seaton Seely Segrave Selby Sexton Shackleford Shanahan Shannon Sharkey Sharkie Shaughnessy Shaw Shay Shea Sheehan Sheridan Sherry Shields Shockency Sholin Short Shortall Silk Simmons Simpson Sinnott Skaggs Skelly Slattery Sligh Sligo Sloan Sly Smiley Smith Smyth Southerland Spaulding Spears Spence Sprague St. Clare Stacks Stanton Stapleton Starnes Staunton Stephens Stewart Stilley Stilwell Stinson Stitt Stockbridge Stone Stoner Storey Story Stover Strong Stroud Sugrue Sulivan Sullivan Supple Sutherland Swanton Sweeney Sweeny Swift

Tallent Tamplain Tatten Taylor Teague Ternney Thompson Thorpe Tierney Tilley Timmons Timms Titterington Toal Todd Tomney Tone Toner Toohey Toohill Toole Toy Tracey Tracy Trainor Trant Treadwell Treat Trent Tressillian Trotter Truesdale Tuhill Tuite Tully Turley Turner Tuttle Tweedy Twomey Tyre Vallely Vance Vaughan Vincent Wade Wakefield Walker Wallace Walsh Ward Wardle Warnock Wasson Waters Waterson Watson Watters Webb Webber Webster Weeks Welch Wells Wellwood Welsh Whalen Whealon Whipkey White Whitehead Whitney Whitt Whittaker Whyte Wiley Williams Williamson Willis Wilson Winchel Winkle Witt Wolfe Wood Woods Wray Wright Wrinkle Wyn

Further Reading and Resources

Books

Aalen, F.H.A. et el (eds), Atlas of the Irish Rural Landscape, Cork University Press, 2011.

Cahill, Thomas, How the Irish Saved Civilization, Sceptre Lir, 1995.

Crowley, Smyth, Murphy (eds), Atlas of the Great Irish Famine, Cork University Press, 2012

Duffy, Patrick, et al (Eds), Gaelic Ireland, c.1250-c.1650: Land, Lordship and Settlement, Four Courts Press, 2001

Duffy, Seán, Atlas of Irish History, gillmacmillan, 1997

Duffy, Seán, The Concise History of Ireland, Gill and MacMillan, 2005.

Duggan, Catherine, The Lost Laws of Ireland, Glasnevin Publishing, 2013

Grenham, J., Tracing Your Irish Ancestors: The Complete Guide. Fourth Edition, Gill and McMillan, 2012.

Hegarty, Neil, The Story of Ireland: A History of the Irish People, BBC Books, 2011

Kostick, Conor, Strongbow: The Norman Invasion of Ireland,

O'Brien, 2013.

MacLysaght, Edward, Surnames of Ireland, Irish University Press, 1973

Mallory, J.P., The Origins of the Irish, Thames and Hudson, 2013

McCaffrey, Carmel and Eaton, Leo, In Search of Ancient Ireland: The Origins of the Irish from Neolithic Times to the Coming of the English, New Amsterdam Books, 2002

McLaughlin and Beattie (Eds), An Historical, Environmental and Cultural Atlas of County Donegal, Cork University Press, 2013.

Neafsey, Edward, Surnames of Ireland: Origins, Numbers and Distribution of Selected Irish Surnames, Rossendale Books, 2012

Nicholls, K.W., Gaelic and Gaelicised Ireland, Lilliput Press, 1971.

O'Croinin, D. (Ed), A New History of Ireland, Volume I: Prehistoric and Early Ireland, Oxford, 2005.

Weir, Mary, Breifne: Chieftain to Landlord, Nonsuch Publishing, 2009.

Online Resources

Your Irish Heritage Blog: www.youririshheritage.com

Your Irish Heritage on Facebook:

www.facebook.com/youririshheritage

Acknowledgements

Almost everything you read in this book has been informed by the questions and stories I have received from our readers over the last two years and our subsequent conversations. I would like to say a huge thank you to all the readers of a Letter from Ireland—it has been such a great journey so far because of this special connection that we have created.

I would especially like to thank the following readers who gave permission to reprint their letters in this volume: Colleen Barrett Lunt, Jack Coffey, Patti Daly, Jane Dougan, Dick Godfrey, Mary Leidner, Pádraic Mac Coitir, Pat Mikels, Barbara Skwarski and Brandy Wilson.

A special thank you to the following eagle-eyed readers who helped with the final layout and offered feedback: Chantel Cummings, Kathleen Flanagan, Terri Makolondra and Tracey Ulrich.

To Ian Armstrong who offered great feedback and final designs.

To Carina who was definitely editor-in-chief when it came to keeping the voice just right and keeping the book readable.

Thank you to all the following people who offered support at a very crucial time:

Alex Cherenko, Andrew Bergin, Ann Ahern Hanson, Ann Marie Battle, Ann Moeding-Evans, Bairbre Gaynor Ryder, Barbara Brogan, Barbara Heffernan, Barbara Olszewski, B.J. Holinka, Catherine Mardon, Cecilia Redmond, Cheryl Bracher, Chuck Real,

184

Acknowledgements

Curtis E. Dooley, Damien Kay, Dana Hurd Zimmerman, Darlene Conner Sampley, Darlene P. White, Dawn Lawry, Debbie Morrill, Deborah Cline, Des Dineen, Dottie Ellsworth, Edward Barrett, Edward Rcidy, Gayle Agren, Gigi, Helen Ward Hancock, The Hendy Family, Hilary J. E. Gordon, Hilary Nic Iomhair, Jack Healey, Jackie Kiley, James Purcell, Jane Dougan, Jane Mackesy, Jim Kenney, Joanne Bednarck, John Coffey, Judy Simmons, Karen A. Hansen, Karen Jarocki, Kate Jamie Peacock, Kathie Vaughn, Kathleen Acker, Kathleen Conlon Sieber, Kathleen Montalbano, Kathleen Sweeney, Kathryn Carrithers, Kerri Follett, Krista Ravenscraft, Lee Ann Walsh, Loraine McMahon, Lucinda Brannaka, Lynda Roddy Ozzauto, Madelaine Singleton, Mandy Gee, Margaret Foster, Margaret Vogtlin, Margery Sudsataya, Marianne Hunnicutt, Marsha McKeown, Marty Frumkin, Mary Kearney Sickler, Mary Leidner, Mary Tarrant, Michael Morgan, Mike Givens, Nickolas McGuire, Noliena Frazier, Pat Murphy-Zezelic, Patricia Barrett, Patricia Hourihan, Patricia Mikels, Patricia Smith, Patricia Underwood, Paul Flynn, Richard O'Mara, Rick Kilduff, Robert O'Laker, Ronald Scanlan, Rosemary V. Baldwin, Sandy Laferriere, Sharon Connor, Sharon Farrell, Sharon Williams Fallstead, Sheila Nelson, Sonia Bax de Keating, Sue Crawford, Teresa R. Shipley, Terri Makolondra, Thomas Lisco, Timothy T. Bourke, Trudy and Art Taylor, Veronica Marie White Sullivan, Vicki Peters, Vincent Walshe, Wayne Cunningham, William Kenealy.

Finally, to the many people who offered very kind feedback, advice and support over the last twelve months.

Thank you! Mike Collins.

Made in the USA
Middletown, DE
06 March 2016